DOSSIER
05

MANAGING FOR KNOWLEDGE

Managing for Knowledge

ACKNOWLEDGEMENTS

This publication was developed by Scitech Educational in partnership with NEBS Management.

Project management: Diana Thomas (NEBS Management)
                        Don McLeod (Scitech Educational)

Series editor: Darren O'Conor

Author: Philip Wilson

Dossier 5:   Managing for Knowledge

A Scitech Educational publication

Distributed by Scitech-DIOL

ISBN 0 948672 87 0

Published by:
Scitech Educational Ltd
15 – 17 The St John Business Centre
St Peter's Road
Margate
Kent CT9 1TE
Tel: +44 (0)1843 231494
Fax: +44 (0)1843 231485
Website: www.universal-manager.co.uk
            http://www.scitechdiol.co.uk

CONTENTS

 MANAGING FOR KNOWLEDGE

THE UNIVERSAL MANAGER SERIES

Books

01 **Risk Management**
02 **Delivering Successful Projects**
03 **Planning and Controlling Projects**
04 **The Learning Organization**
05 **Managing for Knowledge**
06 **Obtaining and Retaining Customers**
07 **Human Resource Planning**
08 **Business Planning**
09 **Financial Performance**
10 **Managing Quality**
11 **Business Relationships**
12 **Managing for High Performance**
13 **Managing Harmoniously**
14 **21st Century Communication**
15 **Managing for Sustainability**

Computer-based Resources

Management Assignments (CD-ROM)
Personal Developing Planning Toolkit
    (**at www.universal-manager.co.uk**)
Learning Styles Toolkit
    (**at www.universal-manager.co.uk**)

 # PREFACE

Today, when internet companies with scarcely any physical capital are sold for £ millions, it is no longer controversial to state that intangible assets have more importance than tangible assets. All organizations possess knowledge, but few even now have the strategy, the systems and the skills to harness and nurture it. As Lew Platt, former Chief Executive of Hewlett Packard, put it:

'If HP knew what HP knows, it would be three times as profitable!'

This dossier is not for the Knowledge Management specialist. It is aimed primarily at the manager relatively new to the concepts of Knowledge Management, perhaps slightly sceptical of the benefits promised by a knowledge-based configuration of organizational processes.

Nor do you need to possess a great familiarity with IT (Information Technology) to make sense of the material provided here. Its purpose is to examine the key principles behind the developing theory of Knowledge Management, and to put forward some practical techniques for effective management of individual and organizational knowledge.

As well as providing a wealth of information for the general reader, *Managing for Knowledge* will support candidates working towards the NEBS Management Diploma and the Management S/NVQ at Level 4.

If you are working towards either qualification, your approved centre will provide guidance on how your study of *Managing for Knowledge* fits in with the overall programme. Appendix 3 of this dossier contains information about the NEBS Management Diploma.

LEARNING PROFILE

Topics included in this dossier are listed below. Use them to make a quick judgement about the level of your current knowledge and understanding, and to highlight the sections of the dossier which will be most useful to you.

KEY	Low	You have never or not recently studied this topic, nor recently applied the concepts at work.
	Mid	You have a broad understanding of the concepts or some experience of working with them, but are not confident about your current level of knowledge.
	High	You are familiar with the concepts and their theoretical underpinning. You could confidently apply the concepts in any work context.

	Low	Mid	High
(1) What is Knowledge Management?			
☛ Understand what is meant by the term 'Knowledge Management' (KM)	❑	❑	❑
☛ Distinguish between explicit and tacit knowledge	❑	❑	❑
☛ Appreciate the importance of a Knowledge Management System (KMS) which is integrated with organizational strategy.	❑	❑	❑
(2) Ownership versus openness			
☛ Identify examples of knowledge assets	❑	❑	❑
☛ Understand how new knowledge can be generated	❑	❑	❑
☛ Understand the ways in which knowledge is codified and transferred	❑	❑	❑
☛ Know how to identify organizational and individual knowledge requirements.	❑	❑	❑
(3) The right culture			
☛ Identify potential barriers to organizational knowledge sharing	❑	❑	❑
☛ Understand strategies for motivating knowledge sharing	❑	❑	❑
☛ Appreciate how people receive, learn and apply knowledge best in the workplace	❑	❑	❑
☛ Understand the competencies required in a knowledge-based organization	❑	❑	❑
(4) KM implementation			
☛ Know how to plan a KM system	❑	❑	❑
☛ Appreciate the impact of KM on customer service	❑	❑	❑
☛ Analyse available knowledge sources	❑	❑	❑
☛ Appreciate the changing nature of organizational communications	❑	❑	❑
☛ Know some important knowledge sharing applications.	❑	❑	❑

	Low	Mid	High
(5) Protecting your knowledge asset			
☛ Know the main legal measures which can be used to protect organizational knowledge	❑	❑	❑
☛ Define and appreciate the application of 'competitive intelligence'	❑	❑	❑
☛ Understand the importance of installing electronic data protection measures	❑	❑	❑
☛ Describe various electronic data protection methods and the threats they are designed to counter	❑	❑	❑
(6) The future of Knowledge Management			
☛ Know how some leading edge organizations are using KM systems	❑	❑	❑ ·
☛ Describe the functions and benefits of Integrated Knowledge Management Systems	❑	❑	❑
☛ Be aware of the ways in which Information Technology is developing	❑	❑	❑
☛ Understand how the business benefits offered by the internet can be maximized	❑	❑	❑
☛ Appreciate how the increasing significance of knowledge for the economy is changing the way organizations and individuals work	❑	❑	❑

www.universal-manager.co.uk

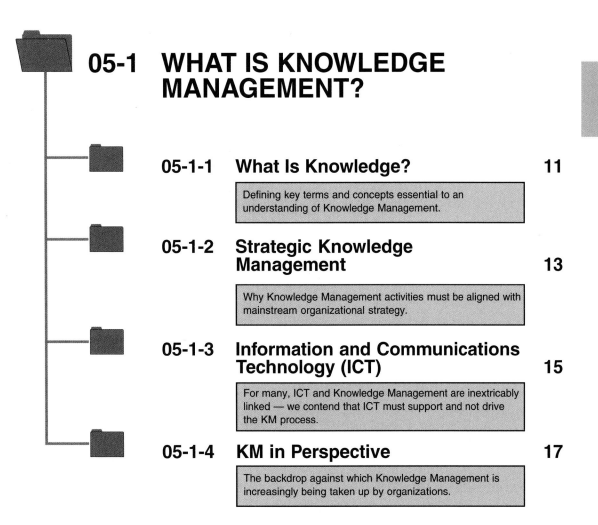

05-1 WHAT IS KNOWLEDGE MANAGEMENT?

05-1 WHAT IS KNOWLEDGE MANAGEMENT?

Knowledge is defined as *'familiarity and understanding gained by experience that is dependent on one's range of information'* (after Concise Oxford Dictionary). The benefits of knowledge to an organization can be likened to those provided by an irrigation system providing life-giving water to arable land. Without water the soil is unproductive — given water and fertile soil, plants will flourish. Like an irrigation system built to collect and distribute water, a Knowledge Management system strives to capture and obtain maximum leverage from 'knowledge capital'.

In essence, an organization wishing to manage its knowledge must:

(1)   Attempt to determine what knowledge is needed;
(2)   Audit what knowledge it possesses;
(3)   Provide a firm basis for knowledge acquisition, development and sharing.

Professor Paul Quintas was quoted in an Open University press release in November 1999 as follows:

> *'Organizations are asking, how do you manage knowing? How do you share knowledge, create knowledge, and begin to value what is in people's heads?'*

It is the job of Knowledge Management (KM) to facilitate these complex and interdependent activities. But whose job is Knowledge Management? With the increasing number of Executive Recruitment advertisements for 'Knowledge Managers' and 'Chief Information Officers', it would be a forgivable assumption that KM is the province of a new and rather mysterious wave of knowledge professionals — nothing to do with the mainstream of management. However, in this dossier we contend that, since managerial activities are all about working with and through people for information acquisition and utilization, all managers must develop the competences needed to utilize KM for maximum organizational benefit.

If organizations need to develop KM systems, senior and middle management must lead by example. Lou Gerstner, CEO of IBM, writing in the first issue of *Connectis*, about the importance of CEOs waking up to the value of the internet:

> *'. . . here is an extraordinarily powerful tool to do the things that you've been trying to do for years, which are to drive down costs, increase productivity, rapidly improve cycle times and speed, create whole new customer relationship management systems.'*

10

He stresses the need to get away from the technological emphasis by moving towards an emphasis on human and organizational benefits, and describes how technology allows global networks to work intensively on a problem:

> *'. . . we can take creative work and have our internal knowledge management network in IBM move that information around the world instantly; we can work on research 24 hours a day, passing it from Beijing to Geneva to New York'.*

A final definition, and perhaps the bluntest summary offered of what Knowledge Management can do for organizations:

> *'. . . the competitiveness of a firm is more than anything a function of what it knows, how it uses what it knows, and how fast it can know something new.' (Davis and Meyer, 1999.)*

05-1-1   What Is Knowledge?

To understand how knowledge can be successfully managed we need to start out with a clear comprehension of what it is. This is not a simple matter. Various interpretations are possible and distinctions are often blurred between related terms such as 'data', 'information' and 'learning'.

 ACTIVITY 1

What would be your definitions of:

(a)   Data

(b)   Information

(c)   Knowledge

(d)   Learning?

Compare your suggestions with ours in the commentary in Appendix 1.

In fact, it may be useful to place knowledge within a hierarchy:

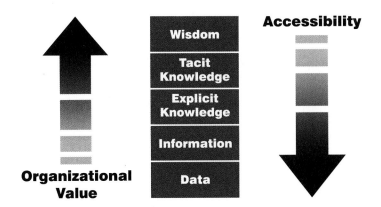

Raw data is easiest to access but meaningless without the application of analytical processes. Wisdom at the top of our hierarchy is the synthesis of knowledge and experience which Knowledge Management Systems strive to tap into: it and Tacit Knowledge reside in the minds of individuals. Knowledge Management is sometimes summarized as the process of converting the top two layers of our hierarchy into Explicit Knowledge.

 PAUSE TO REFLECT

Tacit and Explicit Knowledge are two important terms in Knowledge Management. What do you think they mean?

Now read on.

Tacit Knowledge is information in the minds of individuals, unrecorded know-how accumulated from experience. Explicit Knowledge is information which has been recorded on paper or within a computer file. It is meaningful, and based on understanding and experience.

The human brain has been likened to a container into which information can be poured, and to a sponge because of its capacity to soak up information.

www.universal-manager.co.uk

However, both these analogies are defective — containers fill up and sponges become saturated. The brain has this remarkable and wonderful ability: the more that is put into it, the more it can hold. Learning from appropriate stimulation and experiences ever increases the brain's capacity for more learning, and this in turn increases the ability to process information into knowledge. *Learning organizations* are, in some respects, similar to a human brain. The organization is exposed to a variety of stimuli or data and information (both internal and external) which it processes to produce knowledge capable of being used for the benefit of the organization and its clients.

 ### 05-1-2   Strategic Knowledge Management

Paul Strassman (who has trademarked the term *Knowledge Capital, KC*), in a Knowledge Executive Report in 1996, refers to the need for organizations to consciously turn knowledge assets into competitive advantage. He perceives an organization's KC to be in its people's brains, they have insights into how things work and understand the company culture. Many organizations have very effective KC / KM systems and Strassman cites Coca Cola and pharmaceutical companies such as Pfizer and Abbot Laboratories as good examples. They utilize information management for co-ordination of suppliers, customers and employees. It is also used for managing training, counselling, recording and reporting. Traditionally these are all seen as 'overhead activities'. However, if capital is a manifestation of the accumulation of labour, then KC must also be seen as accumulated labour.

Knowledge Management (KM) systems have been evolving for many decades and identified as a separate 'entity' since the mid-1990s. Many Fortune 500 (USA) and FTSE 100 (UK) companies have realized the benefits of attempting to obtain leverage from KM. Observers in other organizations have seen the benefits accruing to these large, successful corporations and have attempted to emulate them. All too often, however, KM has been seen as a simple add-on, an 'off the shelf' solution. So, rather than being integrated into the organization to become a seamless part of it, new KM systems are imposed by senior management and external consultants. In such circumstances the main beneficiaries have been the (self-publicizing) consultants and providers of computer systems (with their large marketing budgets) rather than the organization that is footing the bill!

If business benefits are to be realized from Knowledge Management, integration of the mainstream business strategy and the strategy for KM is vital. In this sense, the recent vogue in UK business for creating specialist KM roles and departments can be counter-productive — the risk is that the rest of the organization (where the knowledge resides) will see KM as a side issue, not important to their own roles.

Ashley Braganza (1999) of the Cranfield School of Management proposes a framework for linking KM and business strategies founded on four interdependent components:

- ☞ Strategic direction
- ☞ Business processes
- ☞ Knowledge exploitation
- ☞ Knowledge infrastructure.

The first two components should need little elaboration. The plan for knowledge exploitation, Braganza suggests, should be mapped on to each business process and should identify:

☞ Knowledge content
☞ Type of knowledge (whether explicit or tacit)
☞ How information will be shared
☞ Protocols for extracting and transferring knowledge
☞ What organizational changes need to take place in order to carry out the plan for knowledge exploitation.

The knowledge infrastrucure has two essential elements:

☞ *Technological* — the hardware, software and network systems that are required to carry out the plan for knowledge exploitation
☞ *Cultural* — mechanisms introduced to ensure that ownership and adherence to the KM strategy is as wide and as simple as possible within the organization.

Like an effective strategic or business plan, the Knowledge Management strategy should contain impact measures and milestones for review. Measures of KM impact should link the process directly to business objectives

The two essential and interdependent preconditions for effective KM are good management systems coupled with effective Information and Communications Technology (ICT) systems.

 ### 05-1-3 Information and Communications Technology (ICT)

ICT has been and remains the major catalyst of the 'information revolution'. As such, it has both precipitated the need for structured KM systems and is simultaneously an integral part of KM solutions. However, although ICT is an indispensable and essential KM tool, it alone will not solve KM problems nor will it overcome the reluctance of some workers to use computer systems. Similarly, ICT, on its own, cannot overcome the reluctance of workers who are disinclined to share their knowledge.

PAUSE TO REFLECT

The acronym ICT is used widely but loosely. What does it mean for your organization and what types of technology does it embrace?

Now read on.

In general usage, ICT describes the technologies used to communicate information across distances. It therefore embraces network systems from the World Wide Web to the small corporate intranet; familiar communications-based software tools such as e-mail and presentation software; groupware applications such as virtual team working systems; and there is an argument for including specialist packages such as those for accounts, field bus technology, logistics or project management. It certainly encompasses mobile hardware items such as cellphones and laptop computers.

The rapid proliferation of new communications-based technologies with their less than 100% reliability and built-in obsolescence has persuaded most organizations to invest heavily in IT hardware and software. There is a danger, particularly with a discipline like Knowledge Management which is so caught up in the ICT web, that managers will forsake the 'people side' of their function in their attempts to harness increasingly accessible technologies.

But like all management processes, KM is heavily dependent on getting the best out of people. David Guest, Professor of Organizational Psychology at Birkbeck College, London, commented at an Institute of Personnel and Development (IPD) conference in 1999:

> *'Managing people properly translates into profits, so why not do it? Because it's too difficult and inconvenient. They (companies) are much too comfortable with a cost focus and much too busy to concentrate on their people management.'*

By the same token, simply 'throwing money' at ICT solutions is also unlikely to be cost effective. The manager of KM systems must, first and foremost, be a manager of people for, without adequate support or integration of 'knowledge workers', the effect of active KM intervention on the bottom line of a business is likely to be negative rather than positive!

This said, in addition to being a good motivator and having the ability to encourage people to participate in knowledge sharing systems, a KM manager should have a core skill-set in ICT and IS (Information Systems). In a lot of organizations, perhaps even the majority, ICT systems have tended to be the preserve of technophiles — not all of whom have good interpersonal skills (or business management skills).

It is therefore incumbent on the KM specialist, and managers in general, to have an adequate command of ICT. In practical terms this means:

☞ Knowing what the technology can achieve
☞ Being clear about how it can contribute to operational effectiveness and efficiency
☞ Being sufficiently conversant with core technologies to use them according to organizational procedures.

This last point is essentially about setting a good example. There would be no point, for instance, having a company-wide contact database if managers didn't observe company protocols for recording contacts. Without committed leadership, ICT systems introduced to save labour and improve performance can fall into misuse, or worse, abuse.

 ## 05-1-4   KM in Perspective

The backdrop against which most organizations today carry out their business appears to present some telling reasons for adopting a KM system. Here are three:

☞ Although they may not have found their way onto the balance sheet in many companies, intangible assets seem to grow exponentially in value. Hardly a week goes by without an internet company achieving a market value several times that of its book value. This trend has had a few years now to slow down but shows no sign of doing so.

☞ Speed. The speed with which information can now be transferred is one of the defining characteristics of our age, and it too is accelerating. One result is in higher expectations, among customers and colleagues. Knowledge Management is key to meeting the growing expectation for a faster, better quality of information.

☞ Employment trends in the UK suggest a future of increasing change: at industrial level (take-overs, mergers, down sizing) and at individual level (job changing). Retention policies will be crucial for companies wishing to maintain stability, and so will coherent bodies of organizational knowledge.

Another compelling argument for KM is the tendency for excellent companies to practise it: Intel, Microsoft, Ford, Chrysler, BP, Shell, Pfizer, Warner Lambert, Skandia, Texas Instruments . . . the list is as long as it is star-studded! But a note of caution: in 1995, Arthur Andersen & Co surveyed 80 US corporations and found that, while over 75% considered KM essential to business success, less than 10% were able to make direct links between KM and improved financial performance.

Is a structured Knowledge Management system the right thing for you and for your organization? This dossier will help you to decide, but bear the following in mind:

> From a conversation reported in *CIO* magazine (September 15 1997) between Tom Davenport (Director of the Information Management Program at Austin University) and Peter Drucker (Professor at Claremont Graduate School). Davenport, talking about why new management initiatives are constantly being introduced, remarked on the fact that American business is very 'fashion conscious' and that following a trend is a wonderful substitute for thinking! He further commented on the dangerous influence of the gurus and evangelists — organizations must have the courage to ask, 'is this for us?'. In his reply, Drucker concurred that an organization must make a proper diagnosis before it operates and (clearly having no illusions regarding the views of many managers) he concluded, 'to expect a solution from one quick fix is a human failing.'

Although no-one should expect a 'quick fix' from a KM system, evidence does suggest that organizations without a KM system are likely to compete unfavourably against those organizations that **have** developed effective KM. Strassman believes that even commercial giants such as General Motors and IBM were late to recognize and value their Knowledge Capital. For too long, they allowed financial bureaucracy to dominate management and failed to use information to improve what they were doing.

> *'Organizations must overhaul systems to recognize and value KC otherwise they will fail to capitalize on their knowledge assets.'*

 **ACTIVITY 2**

What do you see as the key benefits of KM to your organization?

Note down your ideas in about 50 words.

05-1

Compare your response with our commentary in Appendix 1.

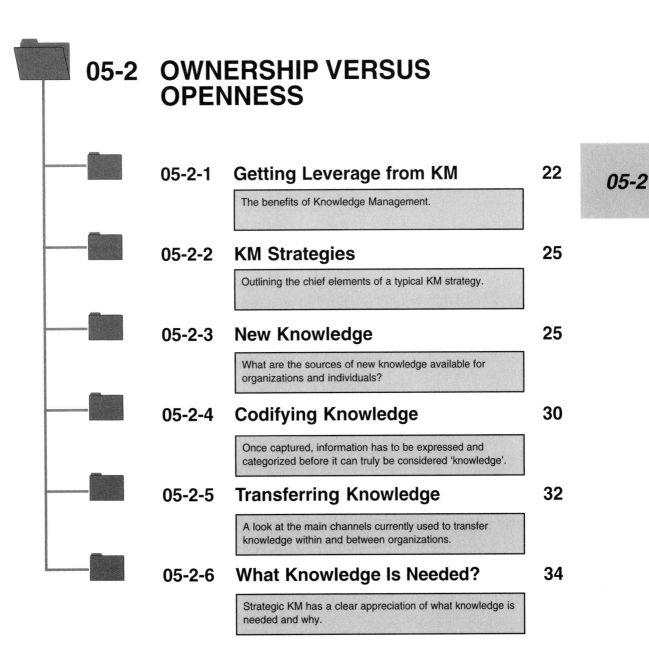

05-2 OWNERSHIP VERSUS OPENNESS

05-2

05-2 OWNERSHIP VERSUS OPENNESS

05-2-1 Getting Leverage from KM

The invention of new terminology and jargon to describe specialized areas of human activities has been with us throughout history. It has always tended to create a clique of specialists who are 'in the know' and who, consciously or unconsciously, have tended to exclude those without the defining skills, knowledge (and ability to use the specialist language or jargon which is essentially a foreign tongue to non-users).

The Jargonese Tribe

Perhaps this apparent need for exclusivity is part of our innate tribalism? Whatever the cause of this non-communication, it has the effect of slowing effective take up of a new discipline like KM:

☛ Factions develop within the 'expert tribe' unable to agree on key concepts and terminologies
☛ The rest of us, the non-experts, will view the new discipline with confusion and perhaps scepticism

The first part of making KM work is to communicate clearly what it means, what it can do and what it involves.

 **ACTIVITY 3**

What examples can you list of knowledge assets possessed by your organization?

Compare your suggestions with our commentary in Appendix 1.

Some forms of explicit knowledge have been valued for a long time in organizations: most businesses standardize and share document formats, operational procedures and work instructions. Knowledge Management goes further by attempting to harness 'collective organizational knowledge'. This is the sum of the learning and experience of all staff and goes way beyond the confines of the technological management of data and information. Traditionally, this 'organizational knowledge' has been concentrated at senior management level and its ownership has been jealously guarded for, as Francis Bacon commented in 1597, *'Knowledge is power!'*.

Those who require information and knowledge must have ready access to it. Without this access, efficient and effective management of the organization is impossible. Consideration must therefore be given to the accessibility of the required knowledge. Is critical knowledge to reside solely in someone's mind (as is all too often the case), or will it be made more widely available in hard copy (as a document, manual or regulations, etc.)? Will it perhaps be held in electronic form as a computer file, letters, databases, spreadsheets? Also, will it be in a central repository or disseminated widely, perhaps via an ICT network? And, what about the security of sensitive data and information? All of these issues need to be addressed within a coherent strategy for KM.

The term 'infonomics' has been coined to describe the interactions of humans with information and IT systems for the processing, interplay, flow or transfer and utilization of information. These are all complex events that are claimed to benefit organizations, but what exactly are these benefits and how can they be measured?

Writing in *CIO* magazine (1 June 1996) Anne Stuart described the perceived benefits of KM in the following terms:

> '. . . fewer mistakes and less redundancy, quicker problem solving, better decision making, reduced research and development costs, increased worker independence, enhanced customer relations, and improved products and services all add up to keep the company a few steps ahead of its competitors.'

In the same article, Leif Edvinsson, Vice President and Director of Intellectual Capital of Skandia Insurance, is quoted as saying:

> 'There is a need to build a bridge between the old ways of doing things and the new ways. Intellectual capital is that bridge.'

However, statements like these are unlikely to persuade those parts of the organization driven by the balance sheet of the actual value of KM. Some attempts have been made to satisfy the need for quantifiable measures, most notably by one of the leaders in KM system development, Teltech.

Teltech uses analysts and databases to help clients define the information and knowledge they require — further analysis is then used to estimate the ROI (Return on Investment) of obtaining that knowledge straightaway. Teltech's calculations for average ROI ratios range from 4:1 in the US distribution industry to 20:1 in the chemical industry. The returns identified come from a wide variety of knowledge applications: directing avenues of research, improving processes and efficiency, avoidance of replicating work or unnecessary investment.

One excellent illustration cited by Teltech comes from Texas Instruments Inc. who claim to have saved $500M by **not** building a new plant — they co-ordinated their intellectual assets to increase productivity in existing factories. The Ford Motor Company's Best Practice Replication system is estimated in one year to have saved the company $34M.

05-2-2   KM Strategies

Most managers, and knowledge managers in particular, recognize that the over-concentration of knowledge can be a barrier to organizational progress and improvement. The purpose of KM Systems (KMS) is to make the organizational knowledge more widely available and utilized, thereby empowering and enabling personnel at all levels to be fully effective in helping the organization to achieve its objectives. KMS attempts to overcome the concentration / dissemination dilemma by a three-part strategy:

05-2

(1)   *New knowledge.* This is generated through learning, research, 'data mining', and ideas development. Managers must be able to recognize what knowledge is required by the organization and develop strategies for its acquisition.

(2)   *Codifying knowledge.* The new and existing knowledge must be in some way codified to make it understandable to the recipient.

(3)   *Transfer of knowledge.* Knowledge transfer or dissemination, to whoever requires it within the organization, is an essential part of KM.

Each of these three components of the KM strategy is discussed in more detail below.

 ## 05-2-3   New Knowledge

Sources of Knowledge

What is 'new knowledge' and how can it be acquired? KM systems usually encourage knowledge workers to carry out active searches amongst sources of existing 'old knowledge'. This is achieved by manual and electronic 'data-mining' of documentation, in libraries, on the Web, in company databases and specialist databases. Efficiency in 'data mining' is improved by good documentation management systems and systems for data gathering and sharing. If used by a good researcher, these methods will usually turn up relevant materials. Very often 'new knowledge' springs from the re-examination or re-evaluation of pre-existing materials.

Peter Drucker (reported in the *CIO* publication, 15 September 1997) is of the opinion that:

> *'Senior management simply do not know what information is available. They need to ask "What information do I need to do my job?". Managers generally understand accounting information but not other sorts; they use lots of internal information but not enough from outside.'*

This general observation is something most managers will sympathize with. However excusable the omission, few managers build in time to their routines for gaining a wider perspective, or even for reflection on work in progress and challenges ahead.

PAUSE TO REFLECT

Take some time to think about:

(a)   The ways in which thinking time might benefit you in your work role

(b)   The external knowledge sources you would like to consult if you had the time.

Most readers should be able to come up with ten items under each of our headings.

The breadth and likely depth of internal information within all organizations calls for systematic analysis. Some examples of internal sources of information are shown in the diagram below.

Internal sources of data, information and knowledge

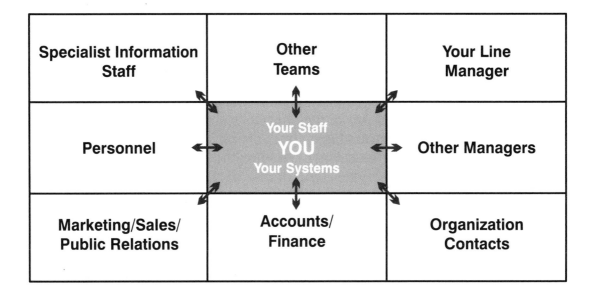

www.universal-manager.co.uk

 **ACTIVITY 4**

In the previous diagram, reference is made to eight internal sources of information that a manager is likely to require to carry out his or her job effectively. Use the blank version below to describe sources of data and information that are required from *outside* your organization for effective performance in your own role.

05-2

External sources of data, information and knowledge

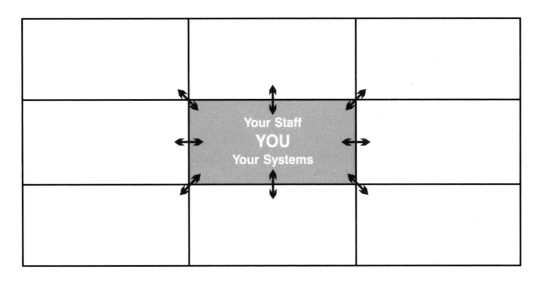

Compare your response with our commentary in Appendix 1.

Acquiring by Sharing

Data mining of a different kind is seen in the learning cultures of many organizations. Here the source of information and knowledge, rather than documentation, is another person's brain. To tap this source of knowledge, and in pursuit of Continuous Professional Development, various HRD (human resource development) activities are undertaken:

☞ Staff attend in-house or external training sessions
☞ Mentoring, shadowing or job swapping may be arranged
☞ Open learning, distance learning, and on-line learning may all play a part
☞ Qualifications are sought
☞ People attend conferences
☞ Staff are tasked with knowledge acquisition projects.

In KM terms, what must be developed, beyond the potentially passive attendance at a learning event, is the skill of evaluating the relevance of the new knowledge to the individual and to the organization. An additional and essential component of this process is the sharing of new knowledge by cascading it through the organization — KM mechanisms must be put in place to ensure that evaluation and cascading occur (these two processes are part of the Investors In People quality model, discussed in Dossier 10, *Managing Quality*).

Acquiring by Buying In

Rather more passive systems for knowledge acquisition can also be employed. For example, the 'buying in' of speciality services can give rapid access to 'instant expertise' and allow the organization to indirectly 'tap into' the experiences of other organizations with whom the provider works. The decision to buy expertise can be finely balanced. It is commonplace in smaller organizations to retain solicitors, accountants, IT maintenance providers and marketing and promotions specialists. In many larger organizations, the last twenty years have seen a degree of vacillation over whether to outsource none-core functions such as training or Information Systems.

 CASE STUDY

A large UK retailer implemented a vast re-engineering programme at the start of the 1990s — as a result, thousands of jobs in administration, training and warehousing were made redundant, many of them at middle manager level.

Subsequently, there was a significant rise in the number of industrial injuries reported in the company. Prompted by this, and by the introduction of new European legislation on Health and Safety, senior management decided that a company-wide safety training programme was needed. A key part of the programme was to be the dissemination of a manual outlining safe working methods for all items of potentially dangerous equipment in use within the organization.

When the appointed consultants came to develop the manual, they found that most of the information they needed on the various equipment models in use had 'left' with the managers made redundant during re-engineering. What should have been a straightforward research and authoring process turned into a series of difficult interviews with embittered ex-employees. The resulting manual was predictably patchy.

This case study is not intended to be a cautionary tale about the perils of re-engineering! But it does illustrate some key points which have a bearing on the decision over buying in expertise:

☞ Employees develop valuable knowledge over time. Their pay and conditions should take into account the value of their expertise (and the cost of losing it).

☞ External agents cannot provide the same understanding of organizational culture and practice. So outsourcing is problematic when the job to be done needs to utilize tacit knowledge.

A related but different form of 'expertise acquisition' is obtained through personnel recruitment — here the acquisition is more permanent and, unless ongoing HRD pertains, the 'acquired expertise' (in the form of the new recruit) can quickly become outdated. This exercise may include 'head hunting' and can be an excellent way to quickly improve the organization's knowledge base and acquire access to a required skill set.

Active Discovery

But what of other more active, 'discovery', methods for the acquisition of new knowledge? In many circumstances the 'scientific method' has considerable value. In this process, a scenario or hypothesis is conceived and tested by analysis and experiment. In many science and technology-based organizations, there is considerable investment in these Research and Development (R & D) activities that form a large part of the knowledge acquisition and development process. A study carried out by the Gartner Group in 1998 showed the pharmaceutical industry as having the highest ratio of intangible to tangible assets.

It is easy to get engrossed in the research and knowledge acquisition processes, but Robert Dunham, President of Enterprise Design, writing in *KM Briefing*, warns and stresses that simply focussing on producing, accumulating and gaining access to information achieves no business benefit. Only effective **action** based on knowledge (from data and information) brings business benefit. He goes on to point out that no amount of hypothesizing and reading around the problem will achieve a solution — effective problem solving can be achieved only by putting ideas into practice.

KM's Metazine (Internet Magazine) states further that, knowledge workers need to know what works, what matters, why it matters, whom to trust, how to fix things, and where to get help. All these factors help to produce an increase in one's capacity to take action.

What sources to use? In addition to the more traditional libraries, organizations are now making greater use of databases of information. Many of these are still paper-based but increasingly, electronic systems are used. When establishing such systems it is usual to utilize SQL (Structured Query Language) software systems.

Most commercial databases — Oracle, Sybase, Infomix, Access and others — use SQL to extract information from tabulated data. Key terms such as 'select', 'like' and 'group by' are used to conduct intelligent searches.

By the use of computer networks, electronic database systems can be accessed remotely and, when properly configured for SQL, complex searches can be carried out and the selected information delivered electronically to the searcher.

 ### 05-2-4   Codifying Knowledge

Records of Utterances

Of course, speech as a means of codifying and transmitting thoughts and ideas remains the most 'normal' means of communication. This means that voice transfer of knowledge (face-to-face, by telephone, by voice mail systems and by tele-conferencing) is particularly effective. However, for KMS there is a major drawback to using voice alone — the ephemeral nature of our utterances.

Technological 'KM tools' can help to overcome this problem. Computers are, of course, important in this area but a great deal of data, information and knowledge can be recorded, codified, transferred and archived by relatively simple means such as pen and paper, word processors, filing systems and photocopiers, fax machines and document handling systems. And, as with any tool, the quality of 'KM tools' lies in their design, their ease of use and in the skills of the tool-user(s) for recording and transmitting information. All these factors act as determinants in the effectiveness of a KMS.

Unified Messaging Systems (integrating voice mail, fax and e-mail) have sprung from the 'voice mail' systems (that developed from simple answer phone systems). Gordon Matthews, who invented voice mail in 1980 is, by his own admission, loved and hated in equal measure.

In the USA, voice mail systems are used more effectively than in Europe. This side of the Atlantic, a British Telecom survey found that 70% of people, when calling a number and hearing a voice mail system simply put down the phone without leaving a message. The 30% that do leave messages mostly record a brief message to say that they have called and ask the recipient to call them back — the resulting ping-pong of messages can be frustrating to say the least. In the USA, the tendency in business is to leave a comprehensive message (often obviating the need for a reply) and for managers to use the group messaging facilities for 'mass-communication'.

The same BT survey found that some people tend to 'hide' behind their voice mail messages and do not answer the phone even when it is ringing at their elbow. Another finding was that most people respond more quickly to e-mail and fax than they do to voice mail. Clearly if the Unified Messaging System is to become a more valuable KM tool (as in the USA), then appropriate staff training is a necessity.

Complex Systems

During the 1980s and 1990s considerable effort was expended in the development of 'expert systems' and these can be helpful in 'automating' routine, formulaic decision making. They cater for such diverse processes as credit rating, medical diagnosis, logistics and the classification of rocks. In the early days of expert systems development, slow computer-processing speed and low memory capacity greatly constrained the effectiveness of these programs. A major problem comes from the inevitable exceptions to general rules, and the consequent difficulty presented to program writers who cannot possibly cover every possibility. With the development of better IT and hardware, there is renewed interest in expert systems and their extension to artificial intelligence (examined in the last section of this dossier).

05-2-5   Transferring Knowledge

John Seely Brown of Xerox, as reported in a 1998 Brint publication, believes that most organizations are ignorant of the ways in which knowledge workers communicate though the social processes of collaboration, sharing knowledge, and building on each other's ideas.

Traditional Communication Channels

Within an organization, knowledge can be perceived as a valuable capital asset and free access to this knowledge is therefore of operational significance. The transfer of knowledge or its dissemination to whoever requires it within the organization, or external to it, is an integral part of KM. Counter to this, excessive bureaucracy is the enemy to the free flow of knowledge.

In many paper-dependent organizations, the use of hard-copy letters, memos, minutes and reports confine data transfer to internal or external postal systems, courier systems and / or fax transmission. Although much improved in recent years (compared, for example, with the days to weeks taken for international transmission of only a few decades ago) surface-mail, air-mail and courier systems have inherent delays that can hold up critical decision-making processes.

'Instant' Communication

In many organizations, 'instant' communication has now become the norm — anything that can be converted into 'digital' form can be transmitted through copper wires, optical fibres or by radio. So, again, ICT has a valuable role to play — it is now commonplace for groups, teams, departments, sections, large sites and nationally or internationally dispersed sites to be linked by computer network systems which thereby remove the time barrier to knowledge sharing. Most systems are 'asynchronous' meaning that information is lodged onto a central server for access by others. Alternatively, 'real-time' or 'synchronous' communication can be achieved when people are 'on line' at the same time. In this situation, communications can be typed, files can be transmitted, also audio and video transmission systems can be used.

Computer networks, Document Management Software (DMS) and groupware (for sharing information) hence provide for the quick, easy and (relatively) cheap sharing of data, information and knowledge. All this, of course, presumes that the knowledge can be somehow codified into an electronic form for transmission and for 're-assembly' by the recipient.

Nowadays, given appropriate technology (and well trained staff who are willing to use it) large and complex documents are scanned or otherwise digitized, transmitted and 're-assembled' by the receiver. Even (small) 3-dimensional objects can be laser scanned and a 3-D facsimile of the object reproduced at the receiving end of the network.

The Downside

Counter to this aim, of keeping personnel fully informed, is the complaint from many managers that they are swamped by information! Estimates show that, on average, managers now spend over 300% more time simply reading and handling information (and concomitantly less time on other tasks) than they did before the 'information revolution' began with the introduction of computers 40 years ago.

Bill Walsh writing in *Game Plan: Blinded by the Byte* (*Forbes* magazine 24 February 1997) coined the term *infolanche*. In summary, organizations come to depend on the gathering and sorting of information. They lose sight of the need to quickly sift through the information to find what is required for decision making. A gut feeling (intuition) is needed for judgement and visionary planning. It is easy to be seduced by the electronic pictures — it is not often the case that if a little information is good then a lot should be even better! Statistical minutiae can obscure the real point so there is a need to find the right information. Without control, there can be damaging consequences because:

(1) The sheer mass of data may support a line of action even though it does not make common sense,

(2) Data can be used as an excuse for bad judgement when things go wrong,

(3) When information becomes the decision-maker, leaders defer decision-making whilst they wait for yet another printout.

So, to avoid burial under the infolanche, have specific priorities of what information is needed, when and how much.

Incoming!

Clearly there is a need for a balance to be struck between the information and knowledge needed by an individual (to efficiently and effectively carry out a defined organizational management function) and that which is simply provided to the recipient 'for information'. Junk electronic communication probably wastes more management time now than junk mail received through the post. An important task of effective KM is therefore development of screening filters to limit the information overload, controlling the intrusion of unnecessary information onto managers' desks and computers, thereby freeing them and their staff to perform more important and more valuable tasks.

 ### 05-2-6   What Knowledge Is Needed?

As part of KM Systems development it is necessary to determine what data, information and knowledge is needed and by whom — this is essentially what Ashley Braganza (1999) terms the knowledge exploitation strategy. In this context, it is likely that distinctions can be drawn between essential knowledge and that which is merely desirable. So, in the context of organizational management, it is necessary for managers to have operational knowledge of:

☞ *The organization's mission, aims and objectives that define its overall purpose.* It appears common for managers, knowledge workers and others to be so engrossed by day-to-day routines and the pressures of their jobs that they lose sight of the prime purpose of the organization. Without this sense of direction it is easy to drift. It is particularly conducive to KM if the organizational strategy defines core competencies (what it is the organization strives to be really good at). A clear definition of core competencies will facilitate identification of knowledge needs.

☞ *People.* In the knowledge-centred organization, people are generally said to be the most valuable asset. In order to leverage maximum organizational benefit from these 'human assets', knowledge managers should have some measure of knowledge workers' value to the organization. One component measure of this may be the competencies and experiences of individuals. A common tactic for integrating KM into mainstream business is to include KM-related objectives in the organizational performance review system. Individual employees may be targetted to generate, apply or share new knowledge in key areas — rewards may be attached to verifiable attainment of KM targets.

☞ *Policies.* These are often used to define the organization's attitudes to significant matters and how these will be managed. Typically, health and safety policy, equality of opportunity and service provision policies will be at the centre of many organizational portfolios. Another important policy may define HRD opportunities.

☛ *Processes*. The key processes performed by the organization need to be mapped from start to finish, to enable a detailed analysis of the knowledge input to each stage of the process. A brief look at just two stages from a typical multimedia development process should underline this point.

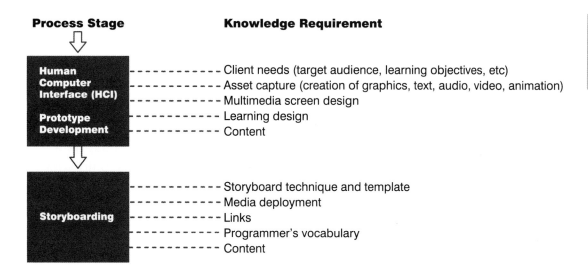

Process Stage   **Knowledge Requirement**

Human Computer Interface (HCI)
Prototype Development
- Client needs (target audience, learning objectives, etc)
- Asset capture (creation of graphics, text, audio, video, animation)
- Multimedia screen design
- Learning design
- Content

Storyboarding
- Storyboard technique and template
- Media deployment
- Links
- Programmer's vocabulary
- Content

☛ *Standards*. Internal and external standards against which the organization is measured by regulatory bodies and customers, for example quality standards such as ISO 9001 for production, 9002 for the service sector and 9014 for environmental protection.

☛ *Operational procedures*. The methods and systems that define how tasks and functions are to be performed often need to be defined. These may, for example, relate to such diverse activities as the safe operation of machinery to financial regulations to the steps to be taken in purchasing items for use within the organization.

☛ *Job specific*. Organizational core competencies may be refined to define the competencies required for key job roles. An alternative is to adopt or adapt off-the-shelf competence frameworks such as are provided by national occupational standards (defined in National Vocational Qualifications and Scottish Vocational Qualifications). Many organizations are actively involved in HRD based on these, or other, standards.

 **ACTIVITY 5**

Competency can be defined as:

$$\frac{\text{skills} + \text{knowledge} + \text{understanding}}{\text{context}}$$

As such, it is difficult to completely isolate 'knowledge' as a separate entity. In this activity you are to attempt to identify the 'knowledge-related' components of the competencies which make up your own job role.

(a)   First, with reference to 05-2-5 and 05-2-6 above, reflect on the data, information and knowledge *that you require from others* to do your job. Some may be 'day-to-day' requirements. Other aspects of knowledge may be required less frequently. Some may be from people in your organization and some may be from people outside it. Brainstorming with a colleague may help you to ensure that as little as possible is missed from your list.

Note down these requirements.

(b)   It may also be of benefit to you to identify and highlight those pieces of data, information and knowledge that you require but which you find difficult to get.

05-2

(c)   Now, reflect on the knowledge *that you yourself must possess* to carry out your job properly and describe this in broad outline.

Now read on.

As a result of the introspection required for Activity 5, you may identify areas of personal knowledge in which you perceive a weakness or deficiency, knowledge that you lack and yet require. In a learning organization this 'gap analysis' should be carried out at appraisal and learning opportunities identified in an Individual Development Programme.

Further, this activity may have helped you to identify specific problem areas where you have difficulty in obtaining knowledge, or areas of personal knowledge in which you perceive a personal weakness.

 **ACTIVITY 6**

If, as a result of working through Activity 5, you have identified gaps in your knowledge, complete the process by devising strategies for acquiring the knowledge you lack.

Now read on.

If you are using this dossier as part of a structured Personal Development Programme, discuss the outcomes of Activities 5 and 6 with your tutor or mentor.

05-3   THE RIGHT CULTURE

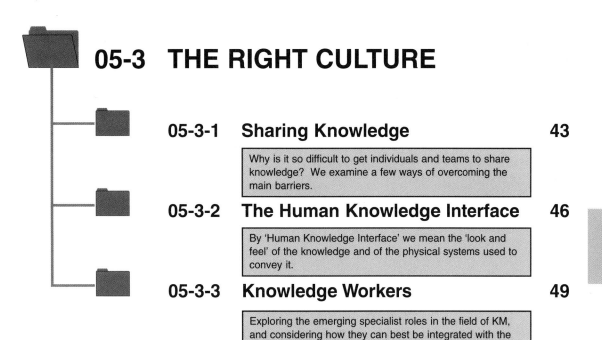

05-3

05-3 THE RIGHT CULTURE

The experience of many successful knowledge-based companies is that achieving the right culture is the hardest part of KM implementation. But without a conducive culture, KM systems will not succeed.

CASE STUDY

A County Council's Senior Management Team decides that Knowledge Management is the solution to its problems of structural fragmentation, inefficiency and patchy performance. A plan and budget are approved by the Members and KM implementation gets underway:

☞ A Chief Knowledge Officer is recruited along with two Knowledge Executives (their brief is to set up a system integrating the IT resources of all units in the County Council)

☞ Details of the new initiative are cascaded via management, departmental and team meetings and a regular column is introduced to the monthly newsletter entitled 'Know How'

☞ A new, state-of-the-art database is commissioned which will be the centrepiece of the new KM system: it will enable staff from all units to enter, download and respond to various categories of knowledge

☞ Training is cascaded down to all staff and volunteers: it centres on practical use of the database but there is some time devoted to explaining KM theory and how it will contribute to improving performance.

After nine months preparation, the new KM system is ready for launch. The results are disappointing:

- ☞ In the first month, the database receives 523 hits (from around 4% of the total full and part time workforce). Of these hits, 214 are entries (to deposit good ideas).
- ☞ Over the next three months only a further 408 hits are recorded of which a mere 73 are entries.
- ☞ 287 innovation ideas may on the surface appear to provide a reasonable 'knowledge pool', but on further analysis this figure contains only 11 recommendations with potential for application beyond a single department or unit, and only a further 18 which could contribute to performance improvement. Most entries are abusive or sarcastic!

An independent audit into why the new system is failing comes up with the following headline messages:

- ☞ Most staff say they are too busy to use the system
- ☞ Many (who attended training) claim not to know how to use it
- ☞ Some state firmly that 'knowledge creation' is not part of their job
- ☞ A few are clear that it would actually be detrimental to their own prospects to give away good ideas
- ☞ The few who have tried the system are not unnaturally disappointed with the results.

Although this is actually a fictional case, it should contain much that resonates with anyone who has been involved in the implementation of a major change programme. In KM terms, it has relevance across many different industry sectors — the same problems have been reported in chemicals companies, financial institutions and NHS Trusts.

The three main cultural barriers featured in our example are encountered time and again by organizations setting out to manage knowledge:

- ☞ The predisposition of individuals, teams and departments not to share knowledge
- ☞ The difficulty of engaging people in new processes, of capturing their attention
- ☞ The 'box' mentality which so often inhibits managers from extending the experience or skillbase of their teams.

In this section we will look at each of these cultural barriers in turn. But first, it is important to be clear about what we mean by 'culture'.

PAUSE TO REFLECT

The illustration at the start of this section hints at a common definition of organizational culture. What would your definition be?

Now read on.

Organizational culture is usually thought to comprise:

☛   **Values** which define what the organization (and its members) is trying to achieve. For instance, an organization may state its intention to become the biggest manufacturer of golf balls in the world. The trick for management is in getting staff to buy into the organization's values.

☛   **Norms** or shared expectations about behaviour in the workplace. In many cases of sexual harassment at work, a key factor is often that the offenders were behaving in accordance with the accepted norm. Another example of an organizational norm would be staying late at the office to complete an urgent task.

☛   **Practices**: the formal and informal ways in which people go about their work. Formal practices will encompass team meetings, checking procedures or time sheets. Informal practices might include office sweepstakes and Friday afternoons in the pub.

Shared values are crucial to any comprehensive change programme such as the introduction of a new Knowledge Management system. But the real values of a collection of individuals are often hard to define, and even harder to alter. David de Long — a fellow of Ernst & Young's Centre for Business Innovation believes that:

> *'Norms and practices . . . are more directly observable and easier for employees to identify. Thus norms and practices around knowledge use are more amenable to change.'*

He goes on:

> *'The most direct way to change behaviours around knowledge use is to change the practices that generate them. New behaviours resulting from new practices will change norms over time . . . . Values are an ever present and powerful force shaping behaviours, but they are usually too complex to change directly.'*

Whether or not we agree with this assessment (and there are many Chief Executives who might dispute the implication that values should not be tackled head on), it is clear that for Knowledge Management to succeed in an organization, there must be an alignment of KM practices and 'the way we do things around here'.

05-3-1   Sharing Knowledge

In essence there are four natural organizational characteristics which mitigate against knowledge sharing between employees in the same organization:

- *Internal competition.* If knowledge is valuable, why should executive A share what she knows with executive B, or team C with team D? Take the example of sales leads — to the individual sales agent they mean commission; to the area sales manager they mean performance bonuses. Sharing those leads would run counter to the competitive culture that sales-based organizations thrive on. But what about cross-selling? Suppose different teams in the organization, responsible for different products, were targetting the same market — it might make more sense to share the leads, but the instinct would be the same. Neither team would want the other damaging its own chances.

- *Internal demarcation.* Linked to the above, but only problematic if there are low levels of trust between different units. It may be that neither values the other's function or performance, or (as is often the case) there may be an overall organizational culture which values one (say R&D) over another (perhaps Finance). It goes without saying that a 'them and us' divide in any organization — whether horizontal or vertical — will hinder performance.

☞ *Narrow focus.* As natural as the tendency to hoard our own knowledge is the inclination not to trust knowledge offered by others. It may be knowledge proven through experience, but it isn't our experience. Receiving it and acting upon it might require changing or even abandoning our own practices — for most of us, the path of least resistance is not to receive it at all.

☞ *Negligence.* Often, failure to share knowledge or to stick to knowledge sharing practices, is not motivated by suspicion or competitiveness at all. It comes about by bad habits which turn into ingrained bad practice. Everyday examples from a typical office might include: not observing the filing system, not entering appointments in the office diary, not recording calls from clients on a contact database. Such small lapses are symptomatic of a wider disregard for the collective or organizational need, be it for accessible files or up to date records.

Altering a culture where sharing is not practised naturally calls for fine judgement over whether to change things wholesale or piece by piece. There is no prescribed approach, but there is a series of tactics which — for best effect — should be employed as part of a single strategy.

☞ *Leading by example.* Whatever the sharing system and whatever the approach to implementing it, expect it to die if managers are not seen to endorse and practise it.

☞ *Measurement.* If knowledge management is considered a core (or desired) competence, it needs to be woven into the organizational system for performance measurement. At Lotus Development, 25% of the performance evaluation of customer support workers is based on knowledge sharing. For total integration, the competence of knowledge sharing should be defined in terms of the skills it requires and the results it should produce; it should be included in job descriptions, and specific performance objectives should be set, ideally for both individuals and teams.

☞ *Structural change.* The 'tear down the walls' philosophy introduced by Chrysler during prototype development of the Viper motor car has gone down in project management folklore. But it is an excellent example of how a small act of cultural engineering can have dramatic impact on performance and productivity (the car was designed in record time and helped re-establish Chrysler on the global market). The essence of it was that the design and engineering teams who had previously worked in isolation, were forced to work together for the duration of the project. Through this experiment they learned what many computer software developers had already discovered: work involving distinct types of expertise will benefit from direct, often intensive interchange between the different domain experts.

☛ *Incentive.* The two types of incentive most established knowledge sharing organizations employ are rewards (usually bonuses payable at certain trigger points for demonstrable and effective knowledge sharing) and recognition (perhaps via employee prizes or an annual conference, which is the practice at Buckman Laboratories in the US).

☛ *Punishment.* Returning to our first tactic, it may be necessary to post one or two 'heads on the gate' to make it unmistakably clear that knowledge hoarding and uncooperative behaviour are no longer permissible. At the very least, it must be understood that no-one will benefit from **not** sharing. It may be necessary to revise the organization's disciplinary policy to make room for penalizing behaviour calculated to undermine knowledge sharing.

05-3

 ACTIVITY 7

Using the four barriers to knowledge sharing, and the five tactics for its improvement, assess the current position of your own organization in terms of:

☛ The obstacles it will need to negotiate in order to bring about effective knowledge sharing
☛ How it is set up for knowledge sharing.

Now read on.

05-3-2   Human Knowledge Interface

Human Knowledge Interface (HKI) is a term we have corrupted from a similar phrase commonly used in computer-based design: Human Computer Interface (HCI). The HCI encompasses all aspects of a computer programme that a user will respond to and make use of to control the package: in essence, the HCI is the 'look and feel' of a programme. Getting the design of the HCI right is crucial to any software or system developer, because if it looks unattractive, or feels awkward, users will reject the programme. The best known example of a HCI is the Microsoft Windows design.

By HKI then, we mean the 'look and feel' of the knowledge and especially of the system for transferring the knowledge. In the case study at the start of this section we described how a large number of staff, trained on a new database system, weeks later stated that they didn't know how to operate it. Anyone who has learned to use a piece of computer software and subsequently never had cause to apply the new skills will sympathize.

The two fundamental requirements of an organization's HKI are that:

☞   It should be easy to use
☞   It should make people want to use it frequently.

Although the analogy with the design of computer screens is a useful one, it should be stressed that the computer is only one medium for knowledge transfer, and arguably one of the least effective for communicating complex or rich information. The two other main mechanisms of course are human contact and paper, but to these could be added audio and video devices.

 ## PAUSE TO REFLECT

Which non-computer-based components might form part of an organization's HKI?

Now read on.

As well as the database, the intranet and the networked project management system, an organizational HKI might employ:

- Regular staff meetings or team briefings
- Brainstorming, snowballing or syndicate sessions
- Internal presentations or demonstrations (perhaps focussing on product or service knowledge)
- Mentoring, shadowing or job swap strategies
- Circulated documents (such as reports or press cuttings)
- In-house libraries.

These conventional devices have certain advantages over computer-based methods. For instance, on-line forums are still several years away from being able to offer the spontaneity and creative interchange that can occur in a well-run brainstorming session; everyone in an organization will know how to use a library but how many can confidently use a search engine; coaching on certain interpersonal skills such as interviewing or delivering presentations will benefit from mixed media (face to face plus video) — a computer-based learning programme could not rival the traditional approach for perception and appropriate feedback.

In short, computers are often not the best medium for presenting or delivering knowledge. They do excel when knowledge has to be transmitted over a distance, or to several people simultaneously, and of course their real strength is the capacity to accurately capture, process and store large amounts of data. But in a HKI, even these abilities are of dubious value without a degree of human filtering.

CASE STUDY

In his 1996 paper 'Some Principles of Knowledge Management', Tom Davenport describes the 'knowledge network of external experts' managed by Teltech. He describes how 'clients who call for referrals are unlikely to always use the same terms as the experts use in describing their work' — a potential problem when clients are requesting information.

Teltech's solution is the Knowledgescope: an on-line search and retrieval system which contains tens of thousands of technical terms, compiled like a thesaurus so that each entry has several synonyms. The system's vocabulary grows with each unrecognized term used by a client, since all 'valid' misses (misspellings are considered 'invalid' and therefore excluded) are added to the database.

The Knowledgescope succeeds because it is designed for use by human beings (not all databases are!) and takes human diversity into account. But diversity is just one difficult human characteristic the successful HKI has to cater for. Two other key human characteristics which any HKI must address are:

☛ *Shortening attention span.* Today, every day is a battle for your attention: newspapers, television, radio, billboards, websites, junk-mail, and e-mail all are part of the infolanche described in section 05-2-5. Increasingly, educational distinctions between media audiences are blurring — the perception is that everyone needs to be instantly engaged by information, otherwise they will switch off. Stark proof of this trend in the UK is provided by the broadsheet newspapers. Compare the cover of today's Times with the equivalent edition 30 years ago: text has reduced by around half; colour and design features such as banners and inlay boxes are used; there are more images. The onus on computer interfaces to engage the attention is even stronger. Text alone is insufficient; text plus graphics won't do; text, animation and audio may not be sufficiently engaging: what matters is the design concept and execution. Screens need to be attractive and stimulating, but simple — too little information is OK, too much is unforgivable. It is no accident that at the leading edge of software design are computer games — many of the ideas and design innovations we will see on the Internet tomorrow are used in computer games now.

☛ *Increasing sophistication.* Partly as a result of the daily media bombardment, we become ever more discerning about the packages our information comes in. After using a search engine which ranks results in order of relevance to the query, we expect the same of every search engine. If one internet provider offers free connection, the rest follow, because the increasingly informed market demands it. At least, this is what the competing sellers would have us believe — in fact, the churn of new offers is now so fast, it is unlikely that such developments are really consumer-led.

There are many other, more complex characteristics which come into play when we 'consume' information: the tension between our instinct for orderly processing of data and our 'surfing instinct' which wants to explore; the need for reinforcement of key messages; the physical discomfort we can feel from spending too long in front of a VDU.

The effective HKI designer will take all of these factors into account and produce a system to deliver information that:

☞ Is presented in an engaging way
☞ Is relevant to us
☞ Is easy to consume
☞ Allows us to explore it as far as we wish
☞ Finally, we will value.

As on-line learning begins to take off in the UK, the biggest challenge for the materials designers will be to create material that lives up to these demanding criteria.

 ### 05-3-3   Knowledge Workers

One dilemma facing organizations opting to embrace the 'knowledge revolution' is to what extent the task of managing knowledge should be specialized, and how far knowledge should become everyone's responsibility.

There is no doubt that the role of knowledge management does demand a set of specific and linked competences, but the dangers in appointing specialist knowledge managers and workers are that:

☞ Unless carefully integrated with the whole organization, the knowledge function may inspire suspicion and actually reduce internal cooperation
☞ The rest of the organization may infer that knowledge gathering and distribution is now a specialist province outwith their own roles.

A good start can be made by specifying knowledge roles carefully and recruiting the right people. The Knowledge Director or Chief Knowledge Officer (CKO) should be responsible for getting the infrastructure in place; facilitating the culture change which will inevitably be needed to make KM work; and ensuring that KM manifestly repays the organization's investment. This calls for a mix of technical knowledge, people skills and bottom line focus which may be hard to find in one person.

Some larger organizations have on their payroll a Chief Learning Officer (CLO) which is a role similar to the CKO but with less emphasis on technical appreciation and more on training and development. The fact that the job is usually in addition to existing HR and Development functions, does however suggest that the CLO will be more concerned with planning and measuring the impact of strategic development than with analysing training needs, or organizing training courses.

Depending, on organizational size, there may be one or more Knowledge Managers reporting to the section head. The Knowledge Manager's role tends chiefly to be about planning and controlling the KM implementation project: systems specification and development; staff awareness and training; monitoring systems usage, etc. So the role calls for project management skills, and a technical IS or IT background.

Matrix Knowledge Management

Many organizations will stop there, reasoning that while there is clear case for extra resources to deliver KM strategy and implementation, operational responsibilities can be integrated within mainstream organizational activities. This is a sound approach provided that alongside what many will view as additional responsibility, staff receive adequate preparation, systems support and incentives to fulfil the KM strategy.

It is important to arrive at realistic picture of the organizational skillset required to manage knowledge at all levels, and assess the extent to which the existing workforce matches up:

☛ KM systems will need maintenance — this may be carried out by the internal IS team, or outsourced

☛ The day to day technical tasks of posting and editing knowledge contributions will probably require familiarity with one or two computing languages (HTML, Javascript and Visual Basic would be typical examples).

☛ To post knowledge effectively, some degree of design skill is important, ideally combined with an appreciation of how people take in and process information

☛ Then there are the knowledge editor/reporter jobs (Andersen Consulting and Ernst and Young have many of these positions) which require an ability to extract knowledge (from people, documents, websites, etc.), structure it and present it to others, and possibly to edit and update it at regular intervals thereafter.

Creating specialist knowledge posts need not result in a lack of ownership among the rest of the organization:

☛ Job specification, selection and induction can be critical here. It is important that specialist knowledge workers at all levels are required to have effective interpersonal skills, and encouraged continuously to relate the work they do to organizational benefits at strategic, team and individual levels.

☛ It is important too to involve as many staff as possible directly in the implementation of KM, through consultation, establishment of cross-departmental teams and in the acquisition and sharing of knowledge.

☛ Finally, and with no apologies for repeating it, performance measurement and related organizational processes must reflect the importance to the organization of managing knowledge well.

05-3

 **ACTIVITY 8**

Using our descriptions of the skills required in effective knowledge workers (at directorial, managerial and operational levels) carry out a quick assessment of your own organization:

☛ To what extent are the required skills available

☛ What strategies might be employed to attain the required skillset?

Now read on.

05-4 KM IMPLEMENTATION

05-4

05-4   KM IMPLEMENTATION

05-4-1   The Framework

Collectively the seven types of knowledge we described in section 05-2-6 form an operational framework in which the knowledge worker functions. In an efficient organization, these 'pieces' of knowledge fit together as in a jigsaw puzzle.

To continue this analogy — the full organizational picture will not be seen if any of the pieces of the puzzle are missing. In a 'learning organization', active steps are taken to develop the breadth and depth of knowledge of all personnel with key staff being targetted for additional support. In order to successfully acquire and utilize operational knowledge, and to begin to undertake the mental shift towards KM, it is therefore necessary to:

(1)   Define clearly the role and functions of the organization or department / team. This can be achieved by a clear definition of mission, aims and objectives. How these are developed is the basis of considerable discussion — it is generally thought advantageous to the 'ownership' of the mission, etc. if it is kept brief, developed collectively and widely disseminated. A frequently encountered problem with such mission statements is that they have a tendency to become 'fixed in stone'. This can militate against the flexibility required in today's rapidly changing commercial environment.

(2)   Define clearly the data, information and knowledge that is required to carry out the organizational function(s). A related aspect of this is to define the task functions required and, from these, define job and / or people specifications. From this functional analysis, every individual in the organization should be able to identify a 'block' of knowledge that is necessary to perform the tasks defined in their job description and, further, to grow in, their job role(s).

(3)   Define clearly the sources and nature of the required data / information / knowledge — who has it, where is it to be found? This includes sources such as journals, texts and databases, refers to key knowledge workers on in-house 'experts', sources from outside the organization and also the 'new' resources of the Web.

(4)   Determine how operational knowledge is accessed by members of a team or department. Will this be from internal and / or external sources? What are the established routes by which operational knowledge is acquired or obtained from these sources and how it will pass to the 'point of use'? Are these established routes efficient or can they be improved?

(5)   Develop systems to verify the accuracy, currency, quality and validity of information received. Erroneous information, late information, information in an inaccessible form, superfluous or insufficient information will seriously limit the effectiveness of the knowledge development and decision making processes (sometimes described as 'GIGO' 'garbage in – garbage out').

05-4

(6)   Maintain the efficiency and accuracy of the data and information (on which operational knowledge is based) by periodically reviewing the acquisition, holding, routeing and checking systems.

Obviously, every organization is different — it has its own unique problems that demand individual solutions. This dossier, although providing general guidance, does not attempt to provide detailed solutions. Instead, it is intended to offer a stimulus by posing questions that must be answered if effective KM systems are to be implemented.

Fundamental Questions

These are some of the fundamental questions that should be addressed at the beginning of KM strategy development:

☞   Which aspects of the organization's mission and aims will be improved by better knowledge distribution, sharing and collaboration?
☞   What is the purpose of a distributed knowledge system?
☞   What are the organizational problems to be solved by KM?
☞   What is it hoped that KM will achieve?
☞   What are the systems to be enhanced?
☞   In what ways is it hoped / expected that the organization will benefit from a KM system?
☞   What difficulties are anticipated?
☞   What are the problems to be solved before KM can be implemented?
☞   What are the resource constraints?

Brain storming, questionnaires, interviews and related techniques can be used to gain access to managers' views — all these processes are standard tools for knowledge acquisition.

Once armed with answers to these questions, formulate clear aims (what is the KM system intended to achieve) and objectives (that define the KM systems' capabilities once complete). Now, the project can begin, or can it?

More Questions

No organization can afford to write an open cheque to fund projects. At an early stage of the planning process it must therefore be decided what resource commitments are planned in terms of:

- ☛ Personnel
- ☛ Budgets and funding
- ☛ ICT requirements
- ☛ Time line
- ☛ Monitoring and review.

 **ACTIVITY 9**

What issues do you think would need to be considered under each of these headings?

Compare your ideas with our commentary in Appendix 1.

The KM Project

With objectives agreed and budgets set, and with responsibilities and lines of control clearly defined, it's time to begin! However, as has been stressed throughout this dossier, successful organizations (and for organizations read managers) are those which are flexible, nimble and adaptable. Despite the best planning, it must be realized that organizations are run by people with the normal spectrum of human frailties — therefore, problems, slippage, etc. should come as no surprise. Some events will be the 'fault' of the project team, others beyond their control. If KM is used as a project tool to develop the project and to keep all informed, then such problems should not cause too much interference with the overall project aims and objectives.

05-4-2   KM and Customer Service

05-4

Customers expect good service, good quality and value — expertise and know-how will help to maintain this. One of the clearest benefits brought by the Knowledge Management approach is in the transfer and presentation to the customer of what might once have been tacit knowledge. Compare these two case studies.

CASE STUDY A

11.15 p.m. on a cold and windswept UK railway station. The 11.03 London train is late. The customer information monitors are blank. A train pulls in and several relieved passengers board it.

When a station employee shouts hoarsely that this is not the London train — some (but not all) of the passengers who have just boarded the train alight. Two of them angrily confront the station employee.

CASE STUDY B

Caradon Everest now equips some of its sales force with laptop computers. These contain adaptable simulations capable of demonstrating to customers what their home will look like with the installation of various Caradon Everest products. The laptops also contain checklists on financing arrangements, and template order forms which the sales agent can complete at the end of a visit and e-mail to Head Office.

These two contrasting examples emphasize two key points about organizations which have embraced Knowledge Management:

☛ They empower employees to find and deliver the information customers want, *when* they want it
☛ They appreciate that customers want information just in time.

Amazon, the on-line book retailer, has an automated expert system for customer service which keeps customers up to date on the progress of their orders. By entering an order number, a customer can check its current status within Amazon's supply system.

05-4-3   Knowledge Acquisition Systems

Where and how does an organization get the data, information and knowledge that it requires? Indeed, how does an organization know what knowledge it requires? Analysis of a typical organization shows that managers obtain their information and knowledge from a large variety of sources, including those shown in the following activity. The relative value of each source obviously differs from person to person.

  ACTIVITY 10

In the table on the following pages, attempt to assess the importance to you of the different sources of data, information and knowledge that are listed. For each source, give a weighting factor between 0 – 9, with 0 having no importance or relevance to you. For those sources that have a low weighting, decide if you need to try to develop this source or could use it to better effect.

Spaces are provided for you to list additional sources.

Source	Value 0 – 9	Comment
Personal memory and experience		
Discussions / conversations with immediate colleagues		
Others in the organization — accountants, purchasing department, ICT department, PR, QC, QA, customer relations		
Meetings (formal and informal / internal and external)		
Conferences		
Courses and other formal learning processes		
Tele-conferencing (audio / video)		
Textbooks and other printed materials in the central library, departmental library, personal library, external libraries		
Specialist publications		
Specialists including consultants		
Trade press		
Directories		
Standards (internal and external)		
Regulatory bodies		
Databases (internal / external)		
'Data mining' the World Wide Web (WWW)		

Source	Value 0 – 9	Comment

Now read on.

05-4-4   Meetings, and Yet More Meetings!

Pre-occupation with creating the ideal learning environment has until recently been the preserve of academic and research-based organizations and even they have been constrained by conventional styles. The debating fora of ancient Rome and Greece are echoed still in the business and board meetings of today. Typically, meetings or conferences involve a number of individuals who come together in order to debate ideas and common interests. Perhaps the meeting has a timetable or a structured agenda, or perhaps a single item for discussion, maybe a series of speeches or lectures followed by questioning and discussion.

Whether or not the meeting can be seen as a 'success' depends very much on who is present and on the perspectives of the participants. Protocol, 'office politics' and social interplay, the organizational status of individuals, the forcefulness or reticence of the participants, their psychological interactions and their strength of feelings all have profound effects on the 'success' of the meeting.

Further, the 'wait your turn' principle necessary to avoid a meaningless babble of voices, probable time constraints, the skills (or otherwise) of the chairperson of the meeting, and the typical 'ebb and flow' of discussion generally means that many, many excellent ideas remain unexplored or underdeveloped. Does the chairperson tease out the views of the most timid and reticent of the participants, who may have considerable experience and insight but dislike sharing their views? Or does the chairperson allow the most assertive person with the loudest voice to dominate the meeting (particularly if that participant is supporting the chairperson's own views!)?

05-4

How are the events to be recorded? Verbatim, minimalist minutes, decisions and action points only — or comprehensive notes? And how will the resultant decisions be disseminated and who will ensure that they are acted upon?

ACTIVITY 11

Over the course of their professional lives, most managers spend hundreds of hours in meetings either as participants or as the chairperson. Some managers would probably suggest that all too many of these hundreds of hours are so much wasted time and that the overall cost-effectiveness of bringing together talented but expensive people is somewhat doubtful.

You have, no doubt, been involved in meetings that were in no way memorable, but many meetings will have been outstanding, some for the right reasons (successful), but others for the wrong reasons (achieved little and wasted everybody's time).

Consider carefully these 'notable' meetings and analyse why some are a success and infinitely more effective than others. Use the prompts shown below, to help you isolate and describe any common factors for success or common factors that cause failure.

Example of *successful* meeting (give date, time, purpose, other features such as chair and participants):

Major factors that made this meeting successful:

(1)

(2)

(3)

(4)

Example of *unsuccessful* meeting (give date, time, purpose, other feature such as chair and participants):

Major factors that made this meeting *unsuccessful*:

(1)

(2)

(3)

(4)

05-4

What, in your power, can you do (or could you have done), therefore to convert 'poor' meetings to successful and effective meetings?

(1)

(2)

(3)

(4)

Now read on.

In the following sections we discuss some of the ways in which the speed and flexibility of knowledge interchange is developing in the 'knowledge age'.

05-4-5   21st Century Meetings

How, in general, can organizations work to improve knowledge development and exchange? For some organizations, the use of teleconferencing has helped to remove some of the logistical and geographical constraints of individual participation. Audio links via the telephone system allow verbal interplay and exchange — sound quality is sufficient to detect nuance and feeling but it cannot, of course, reveal the non-verbal clues of facial expression and body language.

Better, but more expensive, are video-conferencing systems in which video images are streamed between conference rooms over phone lines or via the Internet. Improvements in data transmission speeds and video image compression methods mean that the video images are steadily improving. For global companies and organizations the problems, logistics and expense of getting key individuals to the same place at the same time have largely been eliminated by technology. Only time-zone problems and the desire for 'real time' or synchronous communication limits the usefulness of these methods.

Sorry to keep you waiting Helen, you know
what it's like first thing . . .

 05-4-6   Distributed Knowledge and Groupware

Software programs known as 'groupware' facilitate the sharing of information and knowledge. Sharing means give AND take, NOT simply the accumulation of personal knowledge (that can result in a commensurate accumulation of power). If this situation is allowed to develop, knowledge workers will be reluctant to contribute to online discussions.

The most commonly used 'groupware' packages are Lotus' *Notes* and Microsoft's *Exchange* (and adaptations of them). The protocols and client services of these messaging platforms can be configured to an organization's requirements. Typical groupware functions include collective planning, group diaries and conference areas. However, as has been repeatedly stressed in this dossier, technology on its own will not bring about a knowledge-based revolution. The technology can help but only people can develop the mind-set necessary for active and effective collaboration.

In the 1 March 1996 edition of *CIO* magazine, Carla Paonessa of Anderson Consulting (where the groupware, Lotus Notes, is extensively used), is reported as saying:

> *'You have to celebrate and make visible those who have contributed something that is helpful to you. If you don't put something on the Knowledge Exchange that's valuable, you really don't have the right to take something off it.'*

05-4

To persuade workers to use groupware platforms effectively can, it seems, be difficult. This said, the e-mail functions of these software packages can provide a useful (though expensive), and non-threatening starting point.

Early Computer-supported Collaborative Work

Although synchronous audio and video conferencing has a place in KM, perhaps of greater practical day-to-day value are the systems now in common use for data exchange and computer-supported collaborative work (CSCW). At their simplest, data exchange programs employ the asynchronous e-mail, and 'news rooms' and the slightly more complex real time or synchronous 'chat rooms' of browsers such as Microsoft's Internet Explorer with Outlook Express, or AOL's Netscape Navigator with Netscape Communicator.

WYSIWYG (pronounced wizziwig), 'what you see is what you get' is a phrase used to describe word processor, desk top publishing (DTP) and graphics such as computer aided design (CAD). It refers to the fact that what appears on the VDU, looks the same when printed out.

A development from this has been towards the use of computers for collaborative work. Software that guarantees 'WYSIWIS' (pronounced wizzywiz), 'what you see is what I see' is an essential component in this work. With appropriate technology and software, it does not matter if the collaborators are in the same room, in the same building, or even on the same continent, the technology gives everyone the same view of files that are being worked on and thereby promotes 'object sharing'. These systems are widespread and require only normal computers with 'everyday' software.

More specialized and somewhat more sophisticated are the specialized programs that are devoted to Knowledge Distribution. Described by Michael Schrage (1990), experimental work at Xerox in the late 1980s resulted in 'electronic meetings' in which participants were able to key in their ideas, thoughts, reactions, etc. and ALL statements were shown simultaneously in different frames on a large screen. Removing the constraints of white board, flip-chart, 'wait your turn to speak' and the 'hidden agenda' of many meetings, resulted in rapid developments in:

- ☞ Brainstorming ideas — people can type in what they like without interruption or criticism — ideas trigger new ideas in others.
- ☞ Organizing ideas — sorting, grouping and linking ideas promotes the development of categories and themes. Redundant ideas can be quickly eliminated.
- ☞ Evaluating ideas — ranking them in order of importance, expanding some and demoting others.
- ☞ Generating an outline — onto the above skeleton, the body of development can be grafted. Participants and other interested parties receive a printout of the transactions and discussion threads can be drawn.

Similar work at General Motors in their 'Capture Lab' allowed large screen collaboration and transformed interpersonal interactions.

In both of these examples, it was found that, rather than stifling verbal exchange, the ICT encouraged and improved dialogue, discussion and argument and greatly sped up projects, developments and cycle times.

Modern Computer-supported Collaborative Work

From these relatively crude beginnings, there are now available many sophisticated and user-friendly pieces of software. Seen by many as the business leader in this area, various Lotus products will be used to illustrate the types of software now available for Knowledge Distribution and Knowledge Sharing (groupware). In general, such products are designed to provide high levels of security and to function equally well on a variety of platforms.

(1) *Lotus Notes.* The basic collaborative software with integrated Internet capabilities.

(2) *Lotus Sametime.* As the name implies, this allows users to be aware when colleagues are online (using the Net, searching the Web or e-mailing) and to contact them for instant messaging or for a live 'conversation'. In addition, an object sharing facility allows dispersed users to work on the same document.

(3)   *Lotus Domino Workflow.* Used for the management of processes, procedures and operations on single sites or between distributed sites.

(4)   *Lotus Domino Doc.* Facilitates document management in organizations disributed across several sites. The software allows access to documents by cross-disciplinary teams in distributed workgroups and all drafts are synchronized and held hierarchically in 'a cyber-space filing cabinet' that is available to all in the work-group.

nb This is not to be seen as endorsement of these Lotus products by the author; potential users should research for themselves the current range of similar products currently on the market which include Microsoft packages such as Exchange, Outlook and SQL Server.

Thomas Davenport, reported in *CIO* (1 March 1996) that fewer than 10% of Lotus Notes users fully exploit the collaborative functions (the discussion databases) that are features of the software. So, there are no instant rewards. Davenport thinks that the problems associated with the application of ICT to KM are 95% human and only 5% technological! A counter view might be that if the technology purports to develop our capacity to store knowledge, then the onus is on the programmer and designer to make it easier to do so (and perhaps by implication to make it harder for us to avoid using critical software features).

05-4

Used with appropriate software, the internet is invaluable for linking people in different locations and, in object sharing, for interaction with materials posted on a server. In order to monitor usage and participation, 'hit-rate' counters can be a useful measure of a web site's effectiveness and 'cookies' can help to monitor who uses the site.

And as Michael Schrage (1990) remarked 'Groupware is not a technological solution to an organizational problem. It's a social solution that uses technology to solve an organizational problem'. He also said, 'If you don't have a culture that supports sharing and attribution, then you need to have incentives to do so'. For example, attempts can be made to assess collaborative contributions at appraisal.

In Davenport's article, a different twist is put on the use of groupware by Bruce Hasenyager of AIM Management Group Inc, Houston, Texas — he expresses anxieties for lone 'tele-workers'. 'It's absolutely true that working in groups takes skills and techniques that you don't use in working on your own'. Managers need to inculcate team skills and team processes appropriate for collaborative working, for example, teams need conflict resolution. Lone workers do not need conflict resolution and on-line workers lose the non-verbal clues of tone, pace and body language — lone workers must therefore be supported.

05-4-7   Knowledge Sharing Systems

An organization is under threat of non-sustainability if it allows too much critical information and knowledge to reside solely in the minds of a small coterie of individuals. In purely defensive terms, strategies for sustainability must be established to ensure that the organization becomes less dependent on these key individuals. But systems for sharing knowledge should be viewed not as preventive measures, but rather as potential contributors to strategic success. Properly defined and implemented an effective sharing system can be one of the main sources of leverage for KM. There are now many public examples of effective knowledge sharing. Here are two of them:

Oh, Geoff, oh, Geoff. Where did you put the key to petty cash!

 ## CASE STUDY

The World Bank is known for lending billions of dollars every year to developing countries. Less well recognized is its role in establishing global knowledge-sharing networks which it calls 'communities of practice' (COP). Each community of practice (there are more than 130 at present) centres around a particular field such as road infrastructure or adult literacy, and makes its expertise available to government agencies all around the world. Queries addressed to COPs are quickly circulated among their dispersed members, and expert responses are usually generated within a few days — often they will be followed up by detailed guidance and even visits in person from specialists with experience of the subject at issue.

CASE STUDY

As part of its ISO 9000 implementation initiative, a small Kent-based removal firm has introduced a practice called 'Job Review'. This simply involves the supervisor and crew getting together at the end of each job to discuss how things have gone, and in particular, what difficulties they have encountered. New problems and good ideas are noted, and the MD reviews all notes at the end of each week and circulates a summary of lessons learned. It is a rule that notes and summaries should never be longer than one page.

These two examples may appear to be worlds apart, but they illustrate distinct forms of the same practice: knowledge transfer. The World Bank case is an example of what is termed 'strategic transfer', that is the sharing of complex knowledge which will have a far reaching impact. The case of the removals firm demonstrates 'serial transfer' — a team repeats the same tasks in different contexts and deliberately sets out to learn from each occasion when the task is carried out.

05-4

PAUSE TO REFLECT

Nancy Dixon (2000) of George Washington University identifies five distinct kinds of knowledge transfer. We have met two of them above and the other three are listed below — can you devise approximate definitions?

(a)   Near transfer

(b)   Far transfer

(c)   Expert transfer

Now read on.

It's important to emphasize that these categories are not simply about nice semantic differentiation: they have practical implications for the way knowledge is both transmitted and received. In 'near' and 'far' transfer, the difference is not about spatial distance but more to do with the task to be carried out. *Near transfer* will involve two or more teams in different locations sharing knowledge about the same, usually routine, task to be performed in a similar context. *Far transfer* affects non-routine tasks. A further distinction is that near transfer usually transmits explicit knowledge, whereas far transfer requires tacit knowledge to be shared which may necessitate prolonged, face-to-face contact. *Expert transfer* involves the transmission of explicit knowledge, probably in a standard format and concerning a non-routine task.

 ACTIVITY 12

Can you think of an example demonstrating each of these types of transfer?

(a)   Near transfer

(b)   Far transfer

(c)   Expert transfer

Now read on.

Here are some typical examples:

(a) *Near transfer.* A regional sales force alerts other regions about the emergence of a new, rival product and itemizes its features and benefits on the company intranet. Thus the knowledge, which will be used in routine sales presentations, is made explicit.

(b) *Far transfer.* A building contractor bidding for a large and prestigious contract invites experienced project managers from all of its UK offices to support the lead manager in preparing the proposal. They spend three days cloistered together exchanging tacit knowledge.

(c) *Expert transfer.* An effective on-line 'help' system is an example of expert transfer in action. The user is stuck on a task which he or she rarely carries out, interrogates the system and receives a formulaic response which does not require the sender to interpret the user's exact situation. In Knowledge Management terms, expert transfer has a limited application as anyone who has ever clicked on 'Help' will testify!

05-4

05-4-8   Knowledge Storage and Utilization Systems

Knowledge is available in abundance, the difficulty is in deciding what is really important and then accessing it. Traditionally, libraries have been the main repositories of knowledge. Within large organizations, these are commonly centralized collections of books, magazines, journals, specialist periodicals, papers, documents and reference materials (such as trade directories and telephone directories). In these circumstances, the librarian thus has a pivotal role to play since knowledge storage and retrieval being fundamental to knowledge management. Electronic systems and databases are increasingly used in library systems. Specialist and dedicated software is available for cataloguing, archiving and retrieving. In addition, facsimiles of documents and other materials are now available via computer networks. Such is the belief of some publishers in ICT and the Internet that some technical journals are now available only 'on line' via the Internet.

Local Systems

Within the departments of organizations it is common to find localized libraries of specialist materials. These are held independently of the central library for immediate personal use. Examination of some of these 'local libraries' usually reveals a mixture of resources with some owned by the user and some by the organization but mostly outside the database of the central library. Although much may duplicate what is held centrally, there are likely to be specialized texts, the existence of which should be made more widely known. And herein lies the crux of the problem of knowledge management — sharing!

Centralized Systems

The ever-increasing utilization of electronic computer based systems for communication and knowledge storage / retrieval / transfer / collaborative exchange, etc., with concomitant dependence on IT systems specialists (who may have little concept of management processes), presents particular problems to managers. Perhaps the most important is simply how to understand the complexity of the computer systems and to ensure that they remain a tool of management rather that a constraint or technological barrier.

. . . yeah, you want ms dos, dot exe in 98, control, page up, win ini, insert, dot, colon, back-slash, back-slash, mtx inf, dot, return. Got it?

Also important is the need to avoid being swamped by the avalanche of information. All managers of modern organizations must therefore understand the potential benefits of ICT systems but also the threats they can pose.

To transfer or disseminate information / knowledge to whoever requires it within the organization is one of the major uses of ICT. It is now commonplace for groups, teams, departments, sections, multi-building sites and nationally / internationally dispersed sites to be linked by computer network systems that provide for the quick, easy and (relatively) cheap sharing of data, information and knowledge. The importance of these operations to an organization has spawned an entire industry devoted to the establishment of fast, efficient and secure network systems.

On a practical basis, the processes of organizational information and knowledge flow operates though LANs (local area networks covering a building or a site), WANs (wide area networks controlled by the organization that cover a larger geographical area), the Internet or a combination of these. Secure systems (using passwords, 'signatures' and encryption) enable even sensitive information to be 'posted', questions asked, answers given and knowledge exchanged.

Six Essential Tools

By way of a summary, we will close Section 05-4 with a breakdown of the six distinct but interdependent technology types which go together to make up the complete platform for Knowledge Management.

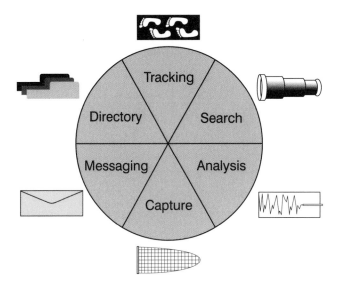

 *Directory.* Typically this will store profile data on either system users, external contacts or both.

 *Messaging* allows people to communicate quickly and store information leading to decision-making. An increasingly popular example is seen in virtual team working systems which allow remote collaborators to share documents, calendars and plans.

 Capture relies upon a widely and well-observed process where team members are aware of what data is relevant to ongoing activities, and know how and where to store new data that they come across or create.

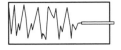 *Analysis* of data may simply involve sorting or categorizing it, or it may require more complex interrogation such as 'what-if' scenarios. Analysis tools are commonly used for identifying business trends and optimum resource allocation or scheduling on projects.

www.universal-manager.co.uk

Search facilities are crucial to the effective usage of KM systems. If indexing or vocabulary are not successfully defined, the entire system will lose credibility fast.

Tracking and associated delivery systems offer functions by identifying the number of times a document is used (which will help to gauge its value and currency) or triggering alarms to remind users of appointments or other key time-related activities.

05-4

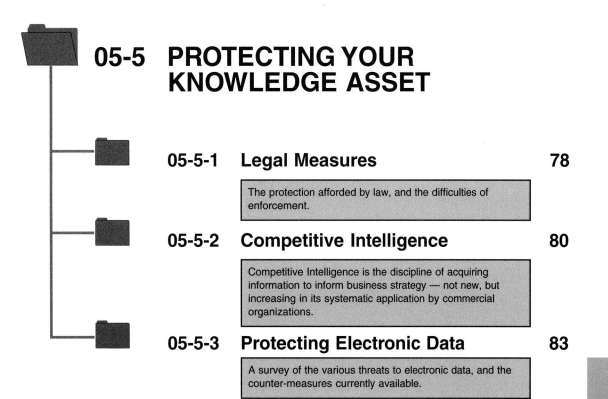

05-5 PROTECTING YOUR KNOWLEDGE ASSET

05-5

05-5 PROTECTING YOUR KNOWLEDGE ASSET

If an organization values its knowledge as a core asset, which sets it apart from the competition, it will surely take steps to protect that asset. In many ways, establishing secure systems runs counter to the empowering principles that underpin Knowledge Management. On the one hand you need to ensure that the organization doesn't leak any of its precious knowledge capital; on the other, you aim to ensure that everyone in the organization can access all the knowledge they need. In this section, we look at some of the tactics organizations can employ to seal in their knowledge assets.

 ### 05-5-1 Legal Measures

There is no formal registration process for protecting trade secrets. But there are many other ways an organization can prevent others from capitalizing on its knowledge asset:

☛ **Copyright** law applies to a tangible and permanent record of knowledge such as a literary work, a film, photograph, or even a performance. It prevents others from copying or reproducing the same work, and does not (contrary to popular belief) require the owner of the work to register it.

☛ **Design right** is commonly used to protect engineering and architectural designs from being copied or reproduced by anyone other than their owners. It also requires the knowledge asset to be made explicit, in the form of a tangible design document for instance, and will protect a design for up to 15 years.

☛ **Patents** do require the knowledge owner to register an idea, and to pay for its protection in named countries for a limited period (usually twenty years). The cost of patenting can be prohibitive particularly to the smaller firm, but one way of securing early revenue from a patent is to license it to third parties.

☛ **Contracts**. Two main forms of contract are worthy of mention here:
    (a) *Employment contracts*. For employees whose knowledge is particularly valuable, it is common practice to use their contract of employment to restrict their ability to work for competitors after contract termination. Many organizations also vary the contracts of employees whose development they have paid for, to prevent them leaving within a specific timeframe.

(b) *Sub-contracting.* Where a sub-contractor will add to or have access to an organization's knowledge asset, it is usual to record a statement of the contractor's rights over that asset. Depending on the arrangement, this may involve stating how the new knowledge will be paid for, agreeing terms such as a royalty payment, or explicitly preventing any reproduction of material created or used during the sub-contractor's work.

PAUSE TO REFLECT

For many organizations, particularly smaller firms, knowing and applying the law presents no real problems. Difficulties can arise when they are called upon to assert their rights. With reference to the protection measures discussed so far in this section, what particular enforcement difficulties might be envisaged?

Now read on.

05-5

The main difficulty is that the enforcement process in cases involving intellectual property tends to be long and expensive. Proving that someone else has infringed on your rights as proprietor of an idea, design or piece of work can be fraught with complexity.

Copyright law, although it prohibits reproduction and 'substantial reproduction by adaptation or translation', is wide open to interpretation (and therefore abuse) on the definition of 'substantial reproduction'. Establishing the line between reference to a work and reproduction of it can be a time consuming and expensive legal process.

Patents may be contested over the issue of scope. To prove infringement, a patent owner will be required to prove that all of his or her original invention, and all of its component parts, has been copied or reproduced without license within a geographical area expressly identified in the patent agreement. Again, the legal process tends to be lengthy.

Employment contracts which seek to lock in corporate knowledge should ideally be in place at the start of the period of employment, and should form part of a package designed to retain the employee and encourage his or her loyalty. As a single protective measure such a contract is unlikely to be effective — in many markets there will be plenty of opportunities for an ex-employee sufficiently committed to causing damage. But proving an ex-employee's collusion with a competitor will not be easy.

Recent years have seen the adoption of a new tactic to counter piracy of corporate knowledge assets — giving the knowledge away! Two quite well-known examples of this tactic in action have been seen in the software development industry.

CASE STUDY

Microsoft's ploy of giving away free copies of Internet Explorer to all Windows purchasers was a calculated move, in the face of intensifying competition on the Internet access market, to make Internet Explorer the *de facto* browser for PC users worldwide.

CASE STUDY

Sun Microsystems went a stage further and gave away an entire programming language — Javascript. The motive — and the result — was the same as Microsoft's. To capture as much of the market as possible by making it easy for anyone to use an asset that Sun had spent years developing.

 05-5-2 Competitive Intelligence

Competitive intelligence (CI) is the collection and analysis of publicly available information that has strategic importance. Strategic information gathering is nothing new, and whether or not it is carried out systematically, most organizations do it. What is new about the emerging discipline of CI is that there is now more intelligence available in the public domain than ever before, and many organizations are dedicating significant resources to capturing it.

PAUSE TO REFLECT

What kind of competitive intelligence is collected by your organization, and what methods are used?

Now read on.

In general, competitive intelligence will be directed towards:

☞ Detecting competitive threats
☞ Eliminating or lessening surprises
☞ Enhancing competitive advantage by lessening reaction time
☞ Finding new opportunities.

It can use information related to almost any product or activity, from a wide variety of sources (private and public sector). CI can be driven by routine information requirements (such as keeping up with the key personnel changes in rival organizations), or important one-off quests (like the need to gather as much information as possible about a new product or service to be launched by a competitor). In fact, CI encompasses all information which may offer some strategic value to an organization: as well as information about what the competition is up to, this will include planned legislation, new government initiatives in employment or training, surveys on consumer spending habits and so on.

In the 'Competitive Intelligence Handbook' produced by Richard Combs Associates, it is claimed that:

'Most of the information needed for a given project is available through publicly-available channels.

The percentage most practitioners place on this kind of public information varies from 80% to 90%. Given the amount of information available in our age, this 80% to 90%, if analysed and presented carefully, can be more than adequate for most needs. The remaining % is insignificant.'

05-5

So where is all this information? Corporate websites often contain a great deal more information than would be published in paper-based annual reports; on-line databases such as Dow Jones and Data Star are invaluable; increasing use is being made of specialist search engines such as www.deja.new.com which tracks on-line discussion groups; business directories like Dun & Bradstreet contain useful data on business size and location; local newspapers (often available on-line) may carry public notices advertising plans for new developments, and it is very common for stories to feature local businesses — a website called www.newslink.org has links to thousands of newspapers and magazines around the world; trade magazines announce new appointments and departures.

Another commentator on CI, Yogesh Malhotra (1996) lists the some typical tools and techniques in his paper ' Competitive Intelligence Programs: An Overview':

- ☛ Contacting government agencies
- ☛ Searching online databases
- ☛ Direct enquiries to competitive companies
- ☛ Surveys and interviews (with selected customers and suppliers)
- ☛ Drive-by and on-site observations (perhaps to view work in progress at a construction site, or to get a snap shot observation of transaction volumes in a rival car show room)
- ☛ Competitive benchmarking
- ☛ Defensive competitive intelligence (monitoring and analysing one's own business activities as the competitors and outsiders see them)
- ☛ Reverse engineering of competing products and services, to identify how they are designed for instance
- ☛ Job applications or offers. For instance, an employee may be sent to apply for a job with a rival firm.

It is important to distinguish between competitive intelligence and corporate espionage — our initial definition of the term stressed that CI is based on information in the public domain. CI does not use illegal methods. That said, it does prey to some extent on indiscretion. It relies on employees who tell the 'customer' a little more than they should, and unguarded web sites still captivated by the internet's ability to communicate in exciting ways to the whole world.

Dreadful results last year, but we reckon this new Artificial Intelligence Unit we're developing is going to clean up . . .

Careless Talk Costs Sales

In fact, given the amount of information about their activities which organizations are compelled to generate and supply (both internally and externally) it is not easy to guard against determined competitive intelligence gathering. Three possible tactics, in descending order of practicality are:

- *Vetting.* Any information for public consumption (web sites, press releases, catalogues, etc.) should be reviewed before release to ensure nothing of value to competitors is revealed
- *Awareness.* All staff who have access to potentially sensitive business information should be made aware of the tactics which may employed to get them to divulge it. (Of course the danger here is of planting the idea of disclosure where it wouldn't normally have occurred.)
- *Misinformation.* A dangerous ploy, but where an organization has a strong suspicion that it is being tracked, false information can be fed out via suppliers, customers and communications.

CI has yet to earn its own section in the UK vacancy sections, but in the US there are a variety of individuals and organizations whose living depends wholly or partly on it. These range from public, legal or corporate librarians and information centre analysts to management personnel, specialists in financial data, business-development people and strategic planners to ex-CIA operatives and retired military intelligence personnel, information specialists and academicians. Suppliers of CI services to industry include research, marketing and public relations firms.

 ### 05-5-3   Protecting Electronic Data

Most organizations have large quantities of information stored in electronic form much of which is commercially sensitive, for example, financial information and market intelligence and personal information (covered by the Data Protection Act 1998). In many cases, too little thought is given to the security of this information.

 ### PAUSE TO REFLECT

What threats are you aware of to the security of information?

Now read on.

One well-publicized security risk is that of 'illegal' entry to corporate IT systems by hackers or by virus infection that can lead to corruption of data. Also, physical vulnerability is common — system damage and data corruption can result from irregular power supplies and more unusual events such as lightning strikes, fire, flood, earthquake, terrorist bombing, etc. all of which must be defended against by contingency or sustainability strategies.

The corruption of data happens most commonly as the result of electronic virus attack. Virus entry into badly managed systems generally occurs via (a) sub-routines of files attached to e-mails and (b) careless or promiscuous use of floppy disks, perhaps used to carry files between home and work or 'private' disks used to ('illegally') load games or screen saver programmes.

Any of these can leave an organization without critical information and knowledge.

Backup Systems

There are many defensive strategies that can be taken to reduce the chances of data and software corruption and some of these are described below. However, due to the relative delicacy and vulnerability of computer systems it is prudent to have backup systems in place that produce duplicates of all essential data. The backup copies are generally held in widely dispersed locations and many organizations have 'fireproof' safes for these critical files and software.

There is a wide choice of backup media available from small floppy disks (which hold only 1.4 megabytes) to writable and re-writable CD-ROMs (holding up to 650 megabytes or more). For general PC use, 'Jaz' drives, 'Zip' drives and similar units provide speed and reasonable capacity. However, most network servers are equipped with multiple 'mirror' hard drives that constantly make duplicate copies of all files and tape streaming systems that can hold many gigabytes of data. The tape backup devices may take a long time to run and are generally set to backup overnight so that, in the event of a system crash, the backup can be used to restore 'start of day' status to the system.

In fact, such is the anxiety of many IT-dependent companies, such as finance houses, that complete mirror IT and office systems are held in readiness in separate buildings.

In a MORI poll (described in *The Times* of 23 February 2000) conducted for the Iomega Corporation, more than half the UK-based IT decision-makers surveyed considered their organizations vulnerable to data theft, while a third would not be surprised to lose data to accidental damage such as a PC being dropped.

Perhaps more worryingly, according to the survey, only 40% of small businesses regularly back up critical files — others rely on the files stored on their hard drive (or are 'just too busy'). Of those that do claim to back up their files, despite advances in high density magnetic media and optical CD storage, nearly two thirds still use floppy disks.

Surprisingly, 14% said they would not suffer any financial loss if they lost all their computer files — but 6% said they would quickly go out of business without their data. If a totally uncontrolled loss of data occurred in the UK's small and medium enterprises, MORI estimates 57,000 companies would go out of business at a cost of nearly £70 billion.

Power Supply Protection

Protection of computer chips and processors can be achieved by the installation of various pieces of hardware. Surges, spikes and sudden power cuts can irreversibly damage computer chips and corrupt software. In-line surge protection devices can be installed to guard against voltage spikes and current surge in mains electricity and in telecom link cables. Uninterruptible power supply (UPS) units (essentially a backup battery system) will protect against sudden power loss and also 'smooth' the electrical current to optimize power supplies.

05-5

Viruses and Hacking

Protection against illegal entry into the system, that may corrupt software, damage files or lead to their theft, is achieved by the installation of anti-virus programs and the creation of 'fire walls' in the system. Viruses attack very commonly through e-mail or the careless installation of software from unchecked sources.

Three lines of defence are usually employed to 'inoculate' systems:

☞ The installation of good quality anti-virus software to detect infection
☞ The creation of 'firewalls' to prevent the spread of infection within the system
☞ The exercise of control over what software is loaded onto the system.

Three lines of defence

Thousands of virus programs are 'out there' waiting to infect your system. Recent killer viruses such as 'Melissa' and the strangely named 'Wobbler' have the capacity to paralyse the victim's hard drive, and render all data on it unrecoverable. 'Back Orifice' which (like many viruses) targets Microsoft Windows, allows the sender to control the infected computer remotely. Like most current computer viruses, these three are communicated by e-mail attachments, and will automatically replicate, sending themselves to all addresses in a victim's address book. It may only be a matter of time before viruses like this can operate independently of e-mail attachments, but while they are confined in this way, vigilant vetting of new mail is at least some defence against infection.

It seems reasonable to ask why evidently talented individuals would expend so much time and energy with the malicious intent of causing grief and inconvenience? A comprehensive explanation would need to explore the complex psychology of the hacker, partly motivated by anti-corporate idealism, and heavily in thrall to his (since the vast majority of hackers are male) own technical ability. If we, in the UK, need convincing of the seriousness of this threat, perhaps we should take note of the fact that the FBI now has a heavily resourced department devoted to countering the threat of hackers and virus programmers.

On the security side, many anti-virus programs are commercially available and, when properly installed, provide considerable protection against virus infection. However, the inventors of virus programs are constantly and assiduously inventing new means of attack and damage. As new viruses become recognized they are examined and the producers of anti-virus software develop inoculation against them. For this reason, it is imperative that anti-virus upgrades are installed on a regular basis. Anti-virus software providers offer an Internet download facility by which regular updates are obtained.

 **ACTIVITY 13**

Which anti-virus software programs are in use in your workplace and is there one procedure associated with running anti-virus software?

Compare your response with our commentary in Appendix 1.

05-5

Physical protection also has a part to play in anti-viral defence strategies. To prevent the loading of 'illegal' software onto a system, lockable inserts can be plugged into disk drives. In some 'thin client' systems, 'dumb' network terminals are used. These have no facilities for software loading and the terminals are dependent on the network server for all their software and for file storage and retrieval. As such, the 'thin client' system is much more secure than the usual networked computers which are generally equipped with floppy disk drives and CD-ROM drives.

Theft

Data in electronic form is relatively easy to steal and very difficult to trace. Various forms of electronic vulnerability exist, for example information can be copied onto floppy disk and carried out of the building; files can be sent over the Internet (perhaps attached to an e-mail) to a third party. Also, hardcopy printouts of computer files and information can be made and carried from the building and photocopies can be made. Theft of web pages or parts of them is a recent development. Efficient web designers now incorporate digital 'watermarks' and encoded text which can be traced by an Internet search and therefore help to establish ownership.

Many knowledge-based organizations (for example government departments, pharmaceutical companies and members of the defence industry) have confidentiality clauses written into staff contracts. Additionally, theft of data in many organizations is usually punishable by summary dismissal and this threat is written into contracts of employment. Access to critical data can also be restricted by the use of strategies such as the use of passwords and the encryption of sensitive data. Physical barriers and lockable drives can be employed to prevent the use of floppy disks and other illegal backup devices. The 'thin client' system may also be of value. Some specific examples of data restriction techniques include:

☞ Personal security systems which enable users digitally to prove they are who they claim to be. Personal and public digital security keys are available from a number of organizations.

☞ A hierarchical password system allows users only into certain permitted areas of the network system. Passwords are changed regularly (and unfortunately forgotten regularly too!).

☞ Protecting organizational documentation and web pages can be helped by the use of a digital 'water mark' or 'metatags' on documents

☞ Protection of mission-critical material by the use of physical and digital 'firewalls'.

☞ Encryption of digital data, where the sending and receiving computers (and no others) hold the digital encryption program and (most important) the de-encryption 'key'.

In addition to these defences, network management software can be configured to monitor and keep a record of all the activities (such as e-mails sent and received, internet usage, etc.) that occur at all the network terminals. By this means, unauthorized usage of the system can, if necessary, be monitored and traced to the offending 'client' pc.

www.universal-manager.co.uk

 **ACTIVITY 14**

(1)   What do you consider to be the main areas of vulnerability of your computer and / or your computer network?

(2)   Indicate possible strategies for minimizing vulnerability.

05-5

Compare your answer with our commentary in Appendix 1.

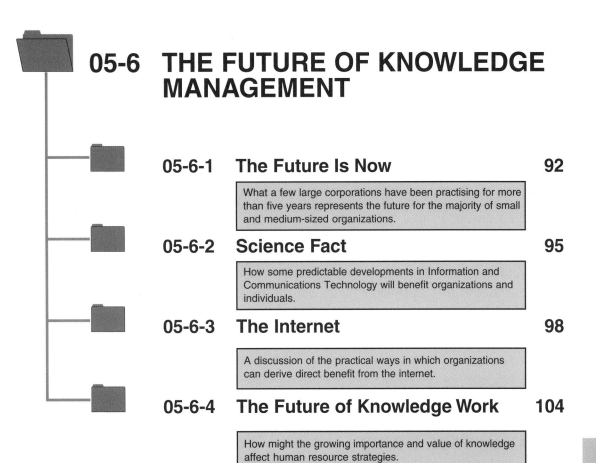

05-6 THE FUTURE OF KNOWLEDGE MANAGEMENT

05-6

05-6 THE FUTURE OF KNOWLEDGE MANAGEMENT

05-6-1   The Future Is Now

For most UK organizations, Knowledge Management **is** the future. Many of the strategies and practices described in this dossier have been developed and refined over the past ten years by leading companies, many of them based in the US, Japan and continental Europe.   It is unlikely that more than 20% of small and medium sized enterprises in this country are practising knowledge management in any systematic way but the discipline is taking root in what might be considered to be unlikely places.

Compare the following brief case studies:

CASE STUDY

The National Police Training Body has a database of good practice in management and leadership. Its purpose is to improve knowledge transfer and performance management among all regional forces, by enabling associations, departments and officers to post and access proven examples of good practice in all aspects of policing.

CASE STUDY

McKinsey & Company uses its Rapid Response Network to enable clients and outposts around the world to quickly tap into its accumulated expertise. The network consists of six consultants strategically stationed to cover all time zones, and two databases, to track requests and to store and locate knowledge resources.

PAUSE TO REFLECT

Approximately ten years separate these two cases. What dates would you put on them?

Now read on.

In fact the first case belongs to the future. It was reported in *People Management* (6 January 2000) and at the time of publication the new database — developed in response to the Macpherson report on the Stephen Lawrence murder enquiry — had yet to be launched. The second case describes one of the first documented knowledge management systems. McKinsey (a leading management consultancy) launched it in 1989 and it has since evolved to the point where it is run by up to ten Knowledge Managers, using a dedicated web site.

The point of this comparison is not to lament the lag between market-leading American firms and UK public agencies, but to emphasize that knowledge management is becoming a mainstream organizational solution. The intent to manage knowledge for the benefit of organizations and their customers is catching up with the technical capacity.

On the technology side, organizations have long possessed the ability to store, categorize and share important data, but now the pace of computer and communications development is widening and strengthening that capacity all the time.

In the short term, we are likely to see and (perhaps) benefit from a number of ongoing developments in the capabilities and usage of Information and Communication Technology:

☞ Faster processors that are smaller, use less power and are cheaper, making portable devices even more versatile.
☞ Better, cheaper memory for RAM, ROM and storage will further improve processing capabilities.
☞ Solid state memory will displace moving media such as magnetic discs and tapes, optical CDs and DVDs — more data will be stored in a smaller space, and be cheaper, easier and faster to access, using far less power and with no moving parts.
☞ Voice and video inter-links with computers will become commonplace.
☞ Language translators for text and ultimately speech (at present 90% of all the millions of Internet pages are in English).

05-6

☛ PCs will disappear to be replaced by hand-held telecommunications devices.

☛ Wireless technology improvements will remove the need for expensive copper and optical fibre based network systems.

☛ The generations who have grown up with the monitor, the mouse and the keyboard will move into the labour market and manual business systems will die out.

In Knowledge Management technology, one of the field leaders is SAP, a German software company which creates sector-specific, integrated systems. Its Knowledge Management system maps key business processes across knowledge development, transfer and content as shown below.

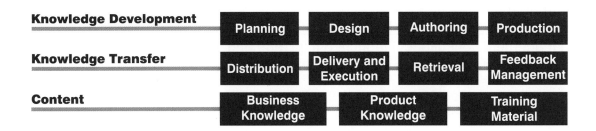

SAP systems offer full integration of internal functions (at individual, team, departmental and site levels) with external interfaces (with customers and suppliers), and the potential for total automation of business processes — the sector-specific organizational process maps are far more detailed than the example shown above.   Given that, in a relatively short space of time, SAP has become the third largest software developer in the world, without any sales to the personal computer market, it is hard not to agree with those commentators who predict that the future of IT is with this fully integrated approach.

05-6-2   Science Fact

Processing Power

Following their widespread introduction into businesses since the mid-1950s, the price of computers has steadily declined and the price per byte of memory of permanent storage and RAM (Random Access Memory) has halved at least every five years. Coupled with this is the ever-increasing clock speed of processor operation. The invention and development of new chip architecture means that processor speed is now measured in hundreds of MHz instead of less than 100MHz in the mid 1990s, and the routine availability of GHz speeds is expected soon.

Faster processing speed, and bigger RAM make it easier for the computer to handle large and complex files (such as high density images, animation or movie files, spreadsheets or databases).

The provision of such power and speed in a machine that is required solely for normal office duties can be seen as expensive and wasteful of capacity. However, more and more desktop machines are being patched into networks to allow information exchange through peer groups or to make them clients of remote servers. However, 'thin clients' are also an increasing trend. In this circumstance, fast processors are useful and good RAM capacity is necessary to rapidly process data for fast uploading and downloading. But, as files are stored on a central network server, large permanent memories are unnecessary.

05-6

Network Speed

An even more critical factor that contributes to communication speeds through networks is the architecture, topology and construction of the network itself. Various standards have been laid down regarding computer network construction and most are installed to various international standards most of which originated in the US. In Europe, installers should work to the CENELEC EN50173 standard (CENELEC is the European Committee for Electrotechnical Standardization). The standard lays down the type of cable and connectors, routing, protection and other factors that influence the maximum speed of transmission.

Transmission speeds are often categorized, for example, Category 4 (or CAT4) can achieve transmission speeds of 10 Mbps (Mega bits per second) but this is regarded as slow. CAT5 allows 100Mbps. CAT5e (i.e. 'enhanced') will run at speeds higher than 100Mbps and CAT6 for 'Gigabit' communications is expected to be introduced during 2000.

Faster transmission speeds make for quicker up- and downloading of files. This will be especially noticeable for graphic images and programs such as the video and audio plug-ins most of us need to play sound or movie files.

Conventionally, copper wires are normally used but these have certain limitations (for example 90m is the normal maximum length allowed), so, more and more of the faster but more costly optical fibre is being used to link components within LANs. Further, the constraints of physical LAN connections are being overcome by microwave and radio links which, although slower and more prone to data corruption than 'hard' connections, are proving useful within multi-building sites.

POPS

The biggest bottleneck to information flow over WANs is the telephone system (POPS = plain old phone system).

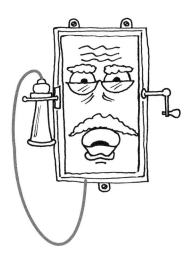

POPS - Plain Old Phone System

Here, instead of transmission speeds being measured in Mbps or Gbps of LANs they are a factor of a thousand or a million times slower (and measured in Kbps for digital signals and kHz for analogue signals, as explained later). Modems, for connection of computers (or fax machines) to the telephone network are rated at, typically 56K or 90K and, although computers are capable of handling far higher speeds, the nature of the phone lines, the telephone exchanges and line 'congestion' severely impede data transmission. Large organizations have partly overcome these problems by using dedicated optical fibre telephone lines but this is a very expensive solution that is outside the reach of most. No doubt research and development will bring about improvements in this situation.

www.universal-manager.co.uk

Artificial Intelligence

Most speculation about the future of Information Technology centres around the likelihood of computers matching or even surpassing human cognitive abilities. Software developers are currently investing heavily in the pursuit of technologies which will go beyond mere labour saving to the point of remembering user preferences and anticipating user needs.

 PAUSE TO REFLECT

Are you aware of any current examples of technology with the capacity to remember or anticipate?

Now read on.

You may have mentioned examples similar to these:

☞ Some e-mail packages are configured to automatically store details of anyone with whom you communicate on three occasions
☞ Many sales websites, having logged your details on the first visit will greet you by name on subsequent visits and suggest options corresponding to preferences established from your previous browsing or buying habits
☞ Word-processing packages are programmed to anticipate certain key phrases in standard documents.

05-6

Despite the great strides that are being made in the area of software development, there is still a wide gulf between artificial and human intelligence. As anyone who has tried it before will appreciate, an excellent demonstration of this gap is provided by speech recognition software.

At the time of writing, no speech recognition software is capable of better than about 85% accuracy. In practical terms this means that, having dictated a letter, you can assume that at least 15% of the text in your document will be wrongly spelt or punctuated. With a short letter, this margin of error is bearable, but with a longer document the time needed for checking and editing threatens to render speech recognition software unusable. As yet, the software is unable to cope with the range of pronunciations, inflections and dialects of which the human voice is capable.

There are many ways to define human intelligence and the work of Gardner (1999) and others on multiple intelligence (MI) suggests that our intelligence results from a number of interactive but separately identifiable components. Nine MI have been identified:

PC Man

- ☛ Logical / mathematical
- ☛ Spatial
- ☛ Linguistic
- ☛ Bodily-kinaesthetic
- ☛ Musical
- ☛ Interpersonal
- ☛ Intrapersonal
- ☛ Existential
- ☛ Naturalistic.

These MI are collectively referred to as our emotional intelligence. The overall intelligence of an individual results from the intimate blending and interplay of these MI and, of course, the ratio of each component in the blend is what gives every individual their unique character, personality and capabilities.

The great leap forward which Artificial Intelligence (AI) has to take is to match the human brain's capacity to bring to bear these MI to work on problems and achieve good results even from incomplete, tentative, partial and probabilistic data. And the factor which may prevent that leap from ever being completed is the complexity of human thought patterns: the sociological and psychological 'baggage' we carry with us and the multiple perspectives from which human problems can be viewed.

 05-6-3 The Internet

Despite the hype, it appears that the internet is not having an immediate major impact on the ordinary lives of most people. On most domestic computers the three most popular Internet pursuits are (a 1999 *Financial Times* survey has shown) viewing 'adult sites', trading stocks and tracing the family tree — '. . . none of these fall into the life transforming category'.

There is no doubt that a transformation is taking place in the financial markets where the value of knowledge or 'context' appears to grow exponentially. But away from the media conglomerates and the software developers, what will the internet do for the small manufacturer, the NHS Trust or the local authority? What is it doing already for your organization?

ACTION **ACTIVITY 15**

(a)   Try to list FIVE practical benefits the internet has delivered to your organization

(b)   Now list FIVE benefits it has offered you in your work.

05-6

Now read on.

Our guess would be that most readers will struggle to list five distinct organizational benefits, and probably have even more difficulty identifying five individual benefits. In fact there are probably four main areas where the Internet offers direct business benefits, but even these are variable:

☛   Acquisition of products or services
☛   Sharing information
☛   Gathering information
☛   Sales and marketing (via a web site).

We will look in more detail at the last two of these potential benefits.

Gathering Information

Estimates suggest that more than 1 million pages are added to the World Wide Web every day. The vast majority are of little interest in KM terms but that still leaves 100s to 1000s a week that may be of value.

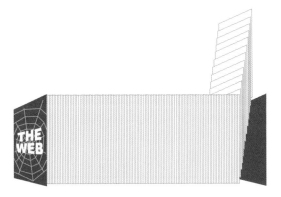

So how do organizations mine this thin but self-sustaining seam of value? First of all they need people who know what to look for and where — this implies a degree of empowerment and ownership (see section 05-3, *The Right Culture*).

They also need accurate and reliable search mechanisms or engines.

At the time of publication, the world wide web is thought to contain approximately 800 million pages. With such a huge, and fast-growing mountain of information, trying to find specific data can be a disheartening experience — many users are discouraged early from undertaking internet searches by the seemingly indiscriminate response to queries.

The solution to this problem is offered by search engines — databases which index web content to make it accessible via key word searches. There is a variety of search engines available and some (such as AltaVista and Google) are provided free with browsers and internet accounts. Despite their vast resources, dedicated to trawling and cataloguing internet content, no single search engine is capable of mapping the web entirely. Conversely, the trouble with linking content to key words, is that relatively common words will cast up thousands of search results, most of which will be of no use to the researcher.

There are no guarantees of finding what you are looking for on the world wide web — any researcher is dependent upon:

☞ Someone posting the required information on a web site
☞ The web site being registered with the researcher's chosen search engine
☞ The key words selected as links to that website coinciding with the researcher's own choice of words (spelled and punctuated in exactly the same way)
☞ The web site and search engine functioning correctly.

100

But by 'intelligent searching', it should be possible for most of us to locate useful and useable information on the 'net. Intelligent searching means using appropriate search engines, and appropriate search language to narrow down the field as far as possible.

Many search engines have their particular strengths and specialisms which the frequent 'net researcher will get to know:

☛ FAST (www.alltheweb.com) is considered to be perhaps the largest with more than 300 million pages indexed in 25 languages
☛ AltaVista (www.altavista.co.uk) is another of the larger engines with its own translation service for searching and reading foreign sites
☛ Google (www.google.com) ranks sites in order of their relevance to the query
☛ Ditto (www.ditto.com) specializes in picture searches
☛ Ingenta (www.ingenta.com) indexes academic journal and articles
☛ Ask Eric (http://ericir.syr.edu) is a research service specializing in educational requests
☛ Metacrawler (www.metacrawler.com) and Ask Jeeves (www.ask.co.uk) will send requests to a selection of large search engines, and display results from all of them.

Search language can become complex, but for the non-specialist, there are some basic techniques which will help isolate relevant search results:

☛ Put double quotation marks around the phrase you are searching for — this signifies that the search should be for the exact phrase with the words grouped as you have typed them (not the individual words used in separate places on a site)
☛ Be precise — if you are searching for data about a particular model of car, use as many qualifying words as you can (e.g. "Ford Escort + 1.8l + ghia + 1998 + burgundy).
☛ Use 'logical operators'. Most databases will understand the plus sign (which means include); minus (exclude); but a more flexible way to cut down or expand your search is to use the three simple words AND, OR , NOT.

05-6

Using Logical Operators (AND, OR, NOT)

AND. Using AND reduces the number of documents retrieved.

> For example, a search on terms pigs AND sheep AND goats would retrieve documents where all of the words pigs, sheep, and goats would appear in **each** document.

OR. Use OR to combine terms that have similar meaning and broaden the search. Using OR increases the number of documents retrieved.

> For example, a search on terms pigs OR sheep OR goats would retrieve documents where at least one of the words, pigs or sheep or goats appeared in each of the documents retrieved.

NOT. Use NOT to eliminate documents containing a specific term.

> For example, a search on terms pigs NOT sheep would retrieve documents on pigs that made no mention of sheep.

 ACTIVITY 16

If you have access to the Internet, try this experiment. Log on and bring up the search facility. Search on the phrase 'Knowledge Management' with no qualifications.

Of course, we don't know what search engine you are using, but the chances are you will have come up with thousands of entries.

Look at two or three at random. The strong likelihood is that your chosen sites will be trying to sell you a product or service — the latest in integrated KM systems perhaps, or a consultancy service.

Now read on.

For those individuals and organizations who profit from the efforts of the rest of us to locate information on the internet, the Holy Grail is to develop a truly intelligent search engine. We are some way from that, but the present and immediate future offer some welcome prospects.

In addition to using the internet as an information source and for 'e-business', 'e-commence' and e-procurement', etc., many large organizations are outsourcing their centralized server hosting. They rent space and bandwidth from a commercial provider onto which data are uploaded and downloaded, via dedicated telecom lines and through which information based systems are managed. This outsourcing to specialist hosting providers is proving a cost-effective solution for many organizations that benefit from the removal of time and geographical constraints. Security is maintained by the use of hierarchical and frequently changed passwords, data encryption, firewalls, and mirror systems.

Business Web Sites

With millions of web users, many companies see the internet as a revolutionary sales medium. However, most web sites are managed by IT personnel (Webmasters) rather than by sales or marketing professionals and, perhaps in consequence, most sites are far from cost effective. Clearly, the synergism of team work between IT support and sales / marketing is essential to attract and hold the maximum number of customers. As part of KM, it is important to realize the need for new management strategies to maximize leverage from the use of the internet. Success in this area (assuming a marketable commodity) is a function of the organization's web site's attractiveness, 'stickiness', interactiveness and ability to maintain customer care by customer communications using e-mail.

05-6

In general, there are three main types of business web site:

☞ The information site — specialist information is provided for those with similar interests.

☞ The promotional site — provides a 'shop window' for marketing.

☞ The sales site — secure site for on-line sales allowing the customer to pay by credit card for goods and services.

Depending on the quality of the brief and the skills of the Webmaster, the sites for e-business, e-commerce and e-procurement, etc. will enhance the organization, but, unfortunately, many sites are rather poor and do not achieve their objectives.

We discuss effective design of business web sites in Dossier 14 of *The Universal Manager* series: *21ˢᵗ Century Communication*.

05-6-4   The Future of Knowledge Work

We have the technology, but so what? Many ICT systems can appear little more than a solution searching for a problem. Organizations must ask themselves what exactly are they trying to achieve? Why embrace the technology, and why make the investments and re-investments necessary to keep up to date? Without direct links to clearly defined strategic objectives and the realistic expectation of sustainable benefits, what motive is there for buying into the communications revolution? Fear of being left behind and of suffering competitive disadvantage may be enough to compel an organization to act, but it will be unlikely to do so systematically and effectively.

If managers need to be clear about what they need to achieve and why, equally they need to know who can help them achieve it. As employment patterns change, with shorter careers and contracts, and an increase in remote working, it will be important for organizations to define who are their (internal and external) knowledge workers; what they contribute; and how to make it easier for them to do so.

Tom Davenport, writing in the *CIO* of 1 November 1999, sees a need for ongoing changes in organizational structure and the identification of 'Key Workers' whose creativity will yield maximum benefit from the application of KM principles. This is only partly to do with the creation of new explicitly knowledge-based jobs (Chief Information Officer, Knowledge Manager and Competitive Intelligence Executive). More significant will be a shift in job analysis and reward structures, where the premium on knowledge contribution should become evident in UK organizations over the next five to ten years.

A related development is likely to be seen in the growth of a knowledge sector: search engine developers, research agencies, and freelance workers combining technical, analytical and presentation skills will be part of this industry. What is hard to predict is the extent to which organizations will outsource their knowledge acquisition and collation: with a growing pool of computerate young graduates to choose from, it may make economic sense to create new positions, particularly as document and system design become more accessible skills.

A final point on the future of KM, again from Davenport. In fact, he is describing the present for those organizations which have spent the last five to ten years developing KM strategies, but the point he makes is one which any company starting out on that journey should heed:

> *'Today, in many companies, the knowledge warehouse is full. In fact one company I know has more that 360 databases and millions of 'knowledge objects.' Its shelves are overflowing and seekers of knowledge are having a difficult time finding what they need.'*

In other words, knowledge is not its own reward. It needs people to put it to work.

05-6

APPENDIX 1

COMMENTARY ON ACTIVITIES

Activity 1

In this dossier, certain assumptions regarding the relationship of data, information and knowledge have been made. Broadly, aspects of the acquisition and assimilation of knowledge can be summarized in the following:

DATA is seen as the raw facts and figures that must be collected and processed to understand what is happening in a system, and:

> *data + context and meaning = information*

So, data processing (the addition of context and meaning) helps to convert data into an understandable form, namely information. Further:

> *information + evaluation with other information = KNOWLEDGE*

It is the application of mental processing that creates meaning from data and information. And also:

> *KNOWLEDGE + intelligence + integrity + motivation =*
> *'good' organizational DECISION MAKING*

Not forgetting, of course:

> *KNOWLEDGE + repeated usage = LEARNING (doing it better next time).*

Activity 2

What you wrote in response to this question is, of course, unique to you and your organization. However, common responses might be:

(1) To enhance internal communication
(2) To facilitate conferencing
(3) So that we can find and supply the information required, when it is required
(4) To improve efficiency
(5) To find out what our customers want and improve customer service
(6) To work better with our supply chain
(7) So that people can't complain about not knowing what's going on
(8) To overcome compartmentalization.

Activity 3

You may have suggested some of the following:

- Patents
- Licences
- Policies and procedures
- Management techniques
- Royalties
- Brands

- Copyrights
- R & D data
- Processes (e.g. for manufacturing)
- Market intelligence and customer data
- Learning materials
- Design rights.

Activity 4

Individuals and organizations external to your own will probably include customers, suppliers, representatives, trade organizations, chambers of commerce, local government, utilities, regulatory bodies, etc.

Activity 9

Personnel

- What are the job descriptions / person profiles of those who will carry out the KM systems implementation project?
- What are the job descriptions / person profiles of those who will maintain the KM systems operation?
- Is outsourcing to consultants to as part of the development and implementation strategy? If so, for what parts?
- Existing personnel — what is their readiness and willingness to support the new initiatives?
- Have the views of existing personnel been sought?
- What are the training requirements for existing personnel (with budgetary implications)?
- New recruitment of specialists — how many, at what level and what salary (with 'on-costs' including office accommodation and ICT)?

Budgets and funding

- Is the scheme to operate within existing budgets?
- Is the scheme to be run from revenue or capital?
- If from capital, will this be taken from reserves or borrowing?
- If capital is obtained by borrowing, how will the debt be secured / serviced?
- Will a separate budget be established?
- Will 'new' money be provided?
- What about year-on-year costs?
- How will ICT hardware depreciation costs be calculated?

☛ How will personnel costs be calculated?
☛ How will consultancy costs be covered?

ICT requirements

Most estimates suggest that the purchase of ICT hardware represents only 20% of the real cost of effective ICT usage by an organization.

☛ What are the ICT hardware requirements?
☛ What are the ICT software requirements?
☛ What are the ICT maintenance estimates?
☛ What are the ICT planned obsolescence / replacement requirements?
☛ What are the ICT training requirements?

Time line

☛ When is it expected that a pilot scheme will begin?
☛ When is it expected that the pilot scheme will finish?
☛ When will the main roll-out begin?
☛ When is it expected that the main roll-out will be finished?

Monitoring and review

☛ What performance indicators will be used to indicate the success (or otherwise) of the KM scheme?
☛ How and when will data / information be gathered for the monitoring and review processes?

Activity 13

Some of the best known anti-virus programs include McAfee, InoculateIT, and Norton SystemWorks. A sensible routine for running this type of software on a standalone or client PC, would be to do it at least once a week and to ensure at least monthly downloads of software upgrades.

Activity 14

You may have ended up with something like this:

Area of vulnerability	Strategies
Poor power supply	Use surge protection and UPS
Viruses	Firewalls and regularly updated anti-virus software
Hackers	Firewalls, passwords, encryption
Theft	Control the use of portable disks; restrict access to data

APPENDIX 2

ICT PLANNING — RESOURCING STRATEGIES

There can be few medium or large organizations without existing ICT (Information and Communications Technology) systems and for these organizations, the following notes may provide a general background for the non-ICT manager. However, for SMEs (small to medium enterprises) that do not have an effective ICT system, the notes will provide guidance for planning a system.

In order to make best use of finite ICT resources, careful planning is required. As organizations have different existing levels of resource, the planning phases and their timing vary considerably. Effective planning is likely to follow the stages below:

(1) PURPOSE / AIMS

These can be summed up in a mission statement that sets out aims and purpose of the ICT system. As in all mission statements there are three components:

(a)   What is to be achieved,
(b)   How it is to be achieved and
(c)   Reference to the type or style of the organization.

(2) RATIONALE

The rationale explains the background and sets out the REASONS why the ICT plans were put in train. Also, it explains the potential BENEFITS and thereby helps to give direction to the planning processes.

(3) POSITIONAL AUDIT

An audit of ICT resource must cover:

(a)   All hardware and its specification (computers, servers, printers, scanners, cameras)
(b)   Software (including licences)
(c)   Infrastructure (network cabling, phone connections)
(d)   Locations for 'a', 'b', 'c'
(e)   Human resources (to include level of confidence and individual experience and training of personnel)

(f)   Preparedness of personnel to use the ICT resources (level of confidence, individual experience and training in its use).

The audit will identify strengths and also act as a 'gap analysis' to reveal weaknesses that are to be addressed by the plan.

(4)   OBJECTIVES

What will be the outcome of the plans? What resources will have been acquired? What will be the usage rates of the resources? What is the time scale involved — what will be achieved in the short term (3–6 months), medium term (6–18 months) and long term (more than 18 months). As technological change is so rapid, long term planning tends to look more at what has to be done rather than how it is to be achieved.

Prioritization of the objectives will also be necessary and it is likely that funding limitations will affect the prioritization process.

(5)   ACTION PLANNING

Like all plans it should be SMART, that is, simple, measurable, achievable, realistic and time bound. The plan must consider the general ICT strategy and look at the following:

(a)   Hardware requirements
(b)   Software requirements
(c)   Infrastructure requirements
(d)   Contract help required
(e)   Training required and who will carry this out
(f)   What ongoing support will be required and by whom.

(6)   IMPLEMENTATION

A spreadsheet with a time line is very useful to define what should happen when — it should also state who is responsible for each stage. A Gantt chart is useful here.

(7)   MONITORING and REVIEW

Formal monitoring is a process of data gathering that is used to ensure 'best value' from the investment. It is necessary to see if implementation plans are successful and if aims and objectives are being met. In a formal review process the results of monitoring indicative outcomes are checked against the aims, objectives and plans. As a result of the consultation and review, revision and re-setting of objectives and plans can be undertaken as required.

www.universal-manager.co.uk

APPENDIX 3

USEFUL RESOURCES

Bibliography / Texts

A Braganza (1999), Developing Knowledge Strategies, *Managing Knowledge in the Digital Age*, an IOD Director's Guide.

W Bukowitz & R Williams (1999), *Knowledge Management Fieldbook*, Financial Times & Prentice Hall.

J Champey (1995), *Reengineering Management, The Mandate for New Leadership*, Harper Business, New York.

R Combs Associates (1999), *The Competitive Intelligence Handbook*, University Press of America.

T Davenport (1997), *Information Ecology: Mastering the Information and Knowledge Environment*, Oxford University Press.

T Davenport and L Prusak (1997), *Working Knowledge, Managing What Your Business Knows*, Harvard Business School.

S Davis & C Meyers (1999), *Blur: The Speed of Change in Connected Economy*, Capstone Publishing Ltd.

N Dixon (2000), *Common Knowledge: How Companies Thrive by Sharing What They Know*, HBS Press.

T M Koulopolos, R A Spinello & W Toms (1997), *Corporate Instinct: Building a Knowing Enterprise for the 21st Century*, Van Nostrand Rheinold.

J Liebowitz (Editor) (1999), *Knowledge Management Handbook*, CRC Press.

D de Long (1997), *Culture Barriers to Knowledge Management*, Ernst and Young.

Y Malhotra (1996), *Competitive Programs: An Overview*, Brint.

H Maturana and F Varela *The Tree of Knowledge*, ('Knowledge is Action').

R L Ruggles (1997), *Knowledge Management Tools*, Butterworth-Heinemann.

M Schrage (1990), *The New Technologies of Collaboration*, Random House.

P Senge (1993), *The Fifth Discipline*, Century Arrow (Business).

T A Stewart (1997), *Intellectual Capital: The New Wealth of Organizations*, Currency/Doubleday.

K E Sveiby (1997), *The New Organizational Wealth: Managing and Measuring Knowledge Based Assets*, Berrett Koehler.

Trevor Young (1998), *The Handbook of Project Management*, Kogan Page.

Specialist journals and periodicals

CIO Magazine

Connectis (a Financial Times e-business publication)

e-Business

Forbes

Journal of Business Strategy

Organizational Dynamics

 Web sites for additional information on KM

Try

Brint organization	www.brint.com
Financial Times	www.ft.com/connectis (FT's e-business magazine)
Forbes Magazine	www.forbes.com
Journal of Knowledge Management Practice	www.tlainc.com/jkmp.htm
Knowledge Management Metazine	www.ktic.com
Knowledge Management News	www.kmnews.com
Knowledge at Work	www.knowledge-at-work.com
Knowledge Praxis	www.media-access.com
Paul Strassman	www.strassman.com
Warwick University	http://bprc.warwick.ac.uk

Internet search engines and portals

Use these for 'information excavation', 'data-drilling', 'data mining'.

To search on single words, type them directly into the search engine text box. To search for phrases and to search for words *exactly* as they appear in your statement, put the words / phrase between inverted commas, " ".

Boolean logic: use the terms OR, AND, NOT, NEAR in your searches to link relationships between search terms (search under 'Boolean logic' for more detailed explanations).

Mathematical logic: use +, – or asterisk 'wild card' expressions in your searches.

Try the following sites:

Yahoo!	www.yahoo.co.uk	the biggest UK system, covers 22 countries
Excite	www.excite.com	has its own directory of over 50M pages
Google	www.google.com	accurate, good for company names
Lycos	www.lycos.co.uk	large system but does not trawl deeply
Altavista	www.altavista.com	claims to be the biggest and fastest
Hotbot	www.hotbot.com	well featured but does not count results
Infoseek	www.infoseek.com	some poor reviews
All The Web	www.alltheweb.com	claims to be the newest and fastest, index of 200M URLs
Northern Light	www.northernlight.com	wide index including books, magazines and news
UK Plus	www.ukplus.co.uk	specializes in reviews of UK sites

The following MetaSearching / MetaCrawler systems assemble pages from several search engines

Try:

Yureka   www.yureka.com

About   www.about.com

Ask Jeeves   www.askjeeves.com

And even the strangely named   www.dogpile.com

APPENDIX 4

GLOSSARY — KM TERMINOLOGY

nb In a fast developing area, consensus on the use of terminology is in constant flux and new terminology is developing all the time. The reader should refer to other sources for more detailed explanations, for example, the Web sites indicated in the 'Useful Resources' appendix above.

BPR	business process redesign
CEO	Chief Executive Officer
CI	competitive intelligence
CIO	Chief Information Officer
CLO	Chief Learning Officer
Groupware	Software program designed to encourage synergistic interchange of ideas and information
ICT	Information and Communications Technology
Intellectual Capital	See 'Knowledge Capital'
IS	Information Systems
Knowledge Capital	the sum total of knowledge on which an organization can draw to obtain leverage
Knowledge Management	structured management systems that maximize organizational benefit from its knowledge capital
Knowledge Workers	those personnel whose main benefit to the organization is in the form of the knowledge they possess and are able to use for the organization's benefit
Re-engineering	originated by Michel Hammer and James Champy; defines the need to change processes, therefore defines the need to reallocate people (who may need re-training); used by many organizations as an excuse to cut costs; seen by many as a largely discredited system.
TQM	Total Quality Management — in which quality is an integral part and formalized part of all systems

APPENDIX 5

NEBS Management Diploma

NEBS Management is the Awarding Body for specialist management qualifications — committed to developing qualifications which meet the needs of today's managers at all levels across industry.

The NEBS Management Diploma is a broad management development programme aimed at practising and aspiring middle managers. It offers a comprehensive, integrated programme of personal and organizational development.

Content

During the Diploma programme, a candidate will:

- Establish a Personal Development Plan
- Study theory and practice in the following key management areas:
    - Managing Human Resources
    - Financial Management
    - Organizational Activities and Change
    - Management Skills
- Produce a specialist Management Report
- Compile an Individual Development Portfolio.

Flexibility

The NEBS Management Diploma requires a minimum of 240 hours of study but can be completed on a full-time or part-time basis as appropriate. Many programmes will offer a mix of direct training, open learning and practical work-based activity. In connection with the Universal Manager series, the Diploma therefore offers the facility for learning in a variety of media including paper-based material, on-line resources and taught elements.

Assessment

Assessment of performance takes a rounded view of the capability demonstrated by the candidate in assignments and specialist tasks, in the management report and portfolio, and in interview.

Enrolment

The usual entry requirements are:

☛   At least two years' relevant management experience
☛   PLUS a NEBS Management Certificate, a Management S/NVQ at Level 3 or the equivalent qualification.

There are many Accredited Centres approved to offer the Diploma programme in the UK and abroad. Call NEBS Management on **0171 294 3053** for details of your nearest Centre.

 # INDEX